NO. 12, SUMMER 1999

NEW DIRECTIONS FOR SCHOOL LEADERSHIP

Partners in Progress

Strengthening the Superintendent-Board Relationship

REBECCA VAN DER BOGERT
Winnetka Public Schools, Evanston, Illinois

EDITOR-IN-CHIEF

MATTHEW KING
Wellesley Public Schools, Massachussets

EDITOR

PARTNERS IN PROGRESS: STRENGTHENING THE SUPERINTENDENT-BOARD
RELATIONSHIP
Matthew King (ed.)
New Directions for School Leadership, No. 12, Summer 1999
Rebecca van der Bogert, Editor-in-Chief

Microfilm copies of issues and articles are available in 16mm and 35mm, as well as
microfiche in 105mm, through University Microfilms Inc., 300 North Zeeb Road,
Ann Arbor, Michigan 48106-1346.

ISSN 1089-5612   ISBN 0-7879-4856-9

NEW DIRECTIONS FOR SCHOOL LEADERSHIP is part of The Jossey-Bass Education Series and is published quarterly by Jossey-Bass Inc., Publishers, 350 Sansome
Street, San Francisco, California 94104-1342.

SUBSCRIPTIONS: Please see Back Issue/Subscription Order Form at the back of this
issue.

EDITORIAL CORRESPONDENCE should be sent to Rebecca van der Bogert,
Winnetka Public Schools, 2759 Eastwood Avenue, Evanston, Illinois 60201.

Jossey-Bass Web address: www.josseybass.com

Printed in the United States of America on acid-free recycled paper containing 100
percent recovered waste paper, of which at least 20 percent is postconsumer waste.

The International Network of Principals' Centers

The International Network of Principals' Centers sponsors *New Directions for School Leadership* as part of its commitment to strengthening leadership at the individual school level through professional development for leaders. The network has a membership of principals' centers, academics, and practitioners in the United States and overseas and is open to all groups and institutions committed to the growth of school leaders and the improvement of schools. The Network currently functions primarily as an information exchange and support system for member centers in their efforts to work directly with school leaders in their communities. Its office is in the Principals' Center at the Harvard Graduate School of Education.

The Network offers these services:

- The International Directory of Principals' Centers features member centers with contact persons, descriptions of center activities, program references, and evaluation instruments.
- The Annual Conversation takes place every spring, when members meet for seminars, workshops, speakers, and to initiate discussions that will continue throughout the year.
- *Newsnotes*, the Network's quarterly newsletter, informs members of programs, conferences, workshops, and special interest items.
- *Reflections*, the annual journal, includes articles by principals, staff developers, university educators, and principals' center staff members.

For further information, please contact:

International Network of Principals' Centers
Harvard Graduate School of Education
336 Gutman Library
Cambridge, MA 02138
(617) 495–9812

Contents

Though a superintendent and a board of education have different roles, if they collaborate as a leadership team they can model the values and behaviors that they espouse for students and staff. A review of the essays in this collection highlights the authors' perspectives on this important relationship.

1

Partners in progress

Matthew King

IN THE SPRING OF 1979, at the tender age of thirty-one, I became a finalist for an administrative position, superintendent/principal of a small K–8 district. I considered myself well prepared for the principal component of the job (since as a teacher I had observed what principals do and had also completed an intensive year-long internship with a superb principal), but the superintendency was a fuzzier concept to me. Yet the board that screened my resume and chose me to be a finalist from among well over two hundred applicants clearly thought I could do the job.

After a grueling day of interviews, beginning with a very early breakfast with two board members, I recall having dinner with two other board members, one of whom filled the space between courses of the meal by asking me how I would approach collective bargaining. Shortly into my response, I saw him begin shaking his head slowly—but horizontally. I knew I had blown the question, and perhaps the job, which I desperately wanted. "No," he said, "that's not right." He then answered his own question for me. *Well,* I thought, *I can kiss this job goodbye.*

NEW DIRECTIONS FOR SCHOOL LEADERSHIP, NO. 12, SUMMER 1999 © JOSSEY-BASS PUBLISHERS

To my great surprise and delight, I was hired. They were seeking someone with limited experience so they would not have to undo what most of their candidates had learned while moving up through the ranks in larger school districts. Indeed, it was my good fortune to land in a district with board members who actually wanted to mentor an inexperienced but malleable young administrator in the role.

As I reflect on the beginning of my career, especially the remarkably supportive relationship I had with my first board, I am struck by how the work of superintendents and principals has become so much more complex, demanding and unforgiving over these past two decades. It is little wonder that at all levels of school leadership across the country there is an acute shortage of people preparing to become, and actively seeking positions as, principals and superintendents. The expectations for us are sky high, the problems are inherently complex, and the political nature of the environment we work in is often very frustrating—and sometimes even treacherous.

I have often felt that one unique perspective on our work is the fact that very few of us consciously decided to become superintendents early in life. Having grown up in an apartment building in New York City, I associated "superintendent" with the fellow who took care of our building! Also, during their formative years, when college students and young graduates mentally try on different careers and professional roles, you will not find many who consider the superintendency. No, those of us in this role invariably began as teachers. Whether it was passion for a subject, enjoyment of learning, fondness for children or adolescents, idealistic commitment to helping make the world a better place, or, as is common, a combination of all of these, we became teachers. I do not know any superintendents who became teachers so that they could become superintendents.

Though their personal journeys as school leaders take many and varied turns, superintendents share deep commitment to students and teachers, and a persistent belief, often in the face of criticism and skepticism, that because of their efforts and leadership both schools and the lives of students are better. The collection of articles in this journal, written by practitioners, explores how we can approach and think about one of the most important, and sometimes most vexing, aspects of school governance: the relationship between superintendents and boards of education. These thoughtful pieces demonstrate that school systems that function well are led by superintendents and school boards who successfully model the values and behaviors they espouse for their students, teachers, and administrators.

In the lead article, Dan Cheever considers the role of boards in our culture and examines the similarities and differences between boards of private and public institutions. Among these differences, I particularly enjoyed reading that even though public boards are more visible and therefore much more accountable to the public, private boards tend to operate in "splendid isolation." It can be argued that introducing cable television to school board meetings has advanced the democratic mission, but those of us who have lived through this transition know all too well that cameras shape how board members address issues, resolve problems, and communicate with each other and superintendents in a way that greatly complicates our work. Yet in the end, based on his extensive experience with boards, Dan believes that the difference between how public and private boards conduct their business is less significant than the quality of the people who serve on boards and, especially, those who serve as chair of a board. Dan's characterization of effective board members and chairs gives us insight into how to create strong, cohesive board-superintendent teams.

For Irwin Blumer, the author of Chapter Three, the art of leadership lies in creating core values and using the superintendent's positional authority to breathe life into them. I believe it was Emerson who first said that "what we do speaks so loudly that no one hears what we say." Irwin presents a compelling case for using the complementary power of words and actions to advance values. Central to his thinking is the idea that leaders must first know what they believe in and stand for before they can expect people to trust them. Without trust, there is little progress toward achieving common goals.

In Chapter Four, Mark Smith notes that "the test of an effective superintendent is often the ability to bring five, seven, or nine board members together rather than keeping them apart." Although this can be a foreboding test of an administrator's patience and skills, effective communication with the board is the sine qua non of effective leadership. Mark believes that whenever possible, superintendents should communicate with the board as a whole and refrain from conducting business through one-on-one conversation with its members. Communication with the board as a whole can be accomplished weekly in writing to convey timely information, offer insights into the superintendent's role, and highlight accomplishments, all of which maintain good morale. Building on these weekly newsletters, Mark goes on to describe how communication and relationship-building can be enhanced through in-person communications during executive sessions, annual planning retreats, and even during the annual evaluation of the superintendent.

Harry Galinsky's career includes working as superintendent, search consultant, and board member. He has learned that skillful school leaders can often overcome very difficult situations with boards and still create a climate of trust and support. To accomplish this, a skillful superintendent needs to adhere to Harry's "Ten Commandments." Though there is nothing new or esoteric in the guidelines found in Chapter Five, seeing them organized as a whole allows us to notice useful connections. When Harry writes passionately about why the superintendent's role is so important and why it is often such a lonely job, he speaks to our hearts: "No matter how close one's associates, how supportive one's board, how understanding one's public and one's family, no one else can fully feel the weight of conflicting expectations, of demands that exceed resources, of the necessity to compromise between ideals and realities. One superintendent once said to me, 'Some days I feel like the only adult in town.'"

In Chapter Six, Betty Twomey contributes a compelling reflection on her years as commissioner of education in New Hampshire. When she took the position, she inherited a dysfunctional relationship between the board of education and the department of education. By "hanging a sign" on this problem and working patiently and consistently with her staff and board, she has been able, over time, to allow genuine dialogue to take place at board meetings. Betty reviews the vast changes that are reshaping the political and cultural landscape of New Hampshire. Amid all these changes, she has demonstrated stable, forward-thinking, and open-minded leadership that enables her to help the governor and the board navigate turbulent political waters.

In the next chapter, Allan Alson writes about how he and his board are facing head-on the underachievement of their minority students in Evanston (Illinois) Township High School, a diverse school of three thousand students. Sparked by a racist incident in 1992, the leadership team—the superintendent and his board—have taken bold steps to address a problem that is largely ignored because of its complexity and the widely held perception that to do so will unleash ugly emotions and reactions that undermine the educational process. Though Allan observes that progress is slow, he also states that "great candor in public discourse provides a glimmer of hope where before there was none."

Rob Evans writes the concluding chapter from the perspective of a consulting psychologist who has spent a career working with teachers, school leaders, and boards. Indeed, I found reading Rob's insightful and wise observations about our work to be highly therapeutic. He has an uncanny ability to see beneath the surface and articulate feelings that go unspoken. His vision of "authentic leadership" is especially useful and ties together a number of the themes addressed in these chapters. His concluding thoughts powerfully capture the opportunity leaders face today:

The truth is that most school leaders have more freedom and leeway than they use. In part this is because the very pressures that are driving people out of the field increase the leverage of those who remain. But it is also because asserting strength builds strength. People everywhere—all of us, teachers, board members, and parents—long to be well led. Not bossed, led. The current climate of school life makes the need for leadership greater than ever. Authentic leaders focused on purpose and conduct are uniquely ready to answer this need in a way that inspires confidence, builds common ground, and gives schools a fighting chance to master the challenges they face.

When I think about the relationship between superintendents and school boards, I am reminded of Tolstoy's haunting introduction to *Anna Karenina:* "All happy families are alike; all unhappy families are unhappy in their own ways." School systems that function well are led by a superintendent and a school board that successfully model the values and behaviors they espouse for their students, teachers, and administrators. If the leadership team does not do this, then time, energy, and resources are drained and redirected into managing the inevitable conflict and miscommunication that result. People in systems enduring this burden experience the unique feelings of unhappiness referred to by Tolstoy. These chapters give useful perspectives on the complexity of school leadership, reinforce the importance of this work, and extend to us a forum for thinking about how we can work more effectively with our boards.

MATTHEW KING *has been superintendent of the Wellesley (Massachusetts) public schools since 1996. Previously, he served as superintendent of Lincoln-Sudbury Regional High School and the Carlisle public schools, all in Massachusetts.*

Although there are significant differences between private and public sector boards, a skillful chair is critical for effective governance of organizations in both sectors.

2

Public versus private boards: Are they different?

Daniel S. Cheever Jr.

WRITING OVER A CENTURY and a half ago, Alexis de Tocqueville described America as a peculiar nation compared to its European antecedents. Among other differences, he noted that in this new land people relied on "voluntary associations" to accomplish many civic purposes. Functions delegated to the church or state in the Old World were handled, in the New World, by formal or informal groups of like-minded citizens. "In no country in the world has the principle of association been more successfully used, and more unsparingly applied to a multitude of different objects, than in America," he wrote, continuing:

Americans of all ages, all conditions, and all dispositions, constantly form associations. They have not only commercial and manufacturing companies, in which all take part, but associations of a thousand other kinds—religious, moral, serious, futile, extensive or restricted, enormous or diminutive. The Americans make associations to give entertainments, to found establishments for education, to build inns, to construct churches, to diffuse books, to send missionaries to the antipodes; and in this manner

NEW DIRECTIONS FOR SCHOOL LEADERSHIP, NO. 12, SUMMER 1999 © JOSSEY-BASS PUBLISHERS

they found hospitals, prisons and schools. If it be proposed to advance some truth, or to foster some feeling by the encouragement of a great example, they form a society.[1]

More than 150 years ago, de Tocqueville saw associations as unique expressions of the democratic ideal in the new land, as a way for citizens to get involved, govern their affairs, and make democracy work. In contemporary times, little has changed . . . except there are more associations. Noted humorist Garrison Keillor has even spoofed about the need for a "National Association of Associations." Keillor may have a good idea. In the Washington, D.C., area alone, 3,686 associations are listed in the compilation of *American Business Information*, and 2,500 are listed in the *Encyclopedia of Associations Geographic Index*. The no-longer-new American democracy is a curious mix of public and private organizations and associations, thousands of them, each designed to advance a specific purpose.

Public and Private Organizations

Despite the growth of government since de Tocqueville's time, private associations are still strong and play a critical role in all aspects of American business, social, governmental, and cultural life. Some of this country's leading research universities, medical centers, and social agencies are privately organized and run. The private business corporation—the great engine of world capitalism today—is essentially a private association that exists to accomplish a business purpose and make money for its shareholders. Like the local church, temple or mosque, hospital, Boy Scout troop, social welfare society, political party, musical group, gathering of do-gooders, or society of combat veterans, the private corporation is governed by a duly elected or appointed board of directors that has ultimate fiduciary responsibility for the furtherance of its purposes.

Private associations flourished at our nation's founding, while later years saw the advance of government agencies or organizations. Today there is a growing return to privatization, a reaction to the extraordinary growth of governmental functions earlier in this century. Beginning in the Progressive Era, accelerating during the New Deal and growing again in the Great Society, government took on provision of services to address important yet unmet social purposes at an unprecedented rate.

Today, many functions formerly handled by private groups are now governmental. Whereas during much of this country's history of charity and service to the infirm was largely a private function carried out by private associations such as settlement houses, today numerous local, state, and federal agencies deliver such services, or funding for them, to fulfill what has become recognized as a public need and public good. Even the arts receive substantial public support at all levels, both through provision of grants to individuals or public or private institutions and through financial support for programs to educate and prepare artists at public or private institutions.

From agriculture to welfare, governmental responsibility for financial support or direct services expanded significantly during much of this century. Only lately has it begun to recede into a "privatized" state. This expansion of governmental functions has grown so large that a decade ago telephone directories in most cities began to reserve separate sections to list local, state, and federal governmental offices. These sections are quite lengthy—twenty-eight pages in the Boston directory alone.

The activity of all these associations, agencies, and groups requires governance. For virtually every type of organization or association, *governance* means a board. Public agencies have governance structures: school boards, city councils, state legislatures, and (ultimately) Congress and the branches of the federal government. Members often are elected, or appointed by elected officials. Private organizations have boards of trustees, boards of directors, or their equivalent. Here, election or appointment usually is by the board itself, which is self-perpetuating, though sometimes all shareholders may vote or ratify. Hundreds of thousands of Americans devote millions of hours of service each year to public or private boards. Indeed, with 15,500 school districts in the United States there may be one hundred thousand volunteers on school boards and countless others on parent-teacher organizations within public education alone. Service on a board of any kind is usually not compensated, and in the case of private boards it often means a financial obligation to donate to the organization as well.

Similarities and Differences

How are public and private boards similar or different? How can each learn from the experience of the other? Are there forms of governance that combine the best of both, or ways of working with either type that can be effective?

There is grave danger of generalizing. With more than thirty-six hundred national private associations represented in the District of Columbia alone, and countless others that are purely local, undoubtedly there is extraordinary difference and variety among them—and even greater variety among the tens of thousands of public organizations and agencies in federal, state, and local governments; large cities; and rural hamlets. What is true for a police chiefs association in Nebraska may or may not be true for its counterpart in Louisiana; what works for the league of women voters in Portland, Maine, may have no relevance whatever to the local United Nations Association in San Diego, California. Nonetheless, there are broad similarities and differences.

First, the similarities. Both public and private boards tend to operate according to defined procedures for the orderly conduct of business. Private organizations generally have bylaws, which set forth the explicit powers and duties of trustees or directors. Public agencies are less likely to codify these practices but are nonetheless governed by past precedent (and hazy remembrance of *Robert's Rules of Order*). Exceptions are regulatory agencies and legislative bodies, both of which tend to have highly detailed procedures for conducting their business. Usually both public and private boards prepare agendas for their meetings, keep minutes, delegate work to subcommittees, and generally operate according to what has been described as "good business practice." They tend to meet on a regular schedule and execute their responsibilities in good faith.

Members of both public and private boards carry a fiduciary responsibility to strive to achieve the organization's aims and refrain from personal profit or conflict of interest. Increasingly, public or regulatory scrutiny has drawn a clearer line as to where fiduciary responsibility begins and personal profit must end. In Massachusetts, for example, the attorney general recently launched an aggressive investigation of alleged or potential conflicts of interest on the part of certain members of the board of trustees of a major research university who also had business relationships with the same university. The attorney general further questioned the university's significant investment in a biotech start-up company and the potential overlap of roles among the company's board of directors and certain university officials. Similar issues at a major university in New York eventually prompted the state's board of regents to remove and replace almost all the members of the board of trustees—and the university president.

Faithful adherence to fiduciary responsibility and avoidance of conflict of interest are becoming stringent standards, particularly for members of private boards. For years, those serving on the board of a public agency were likely to follow these standards in part because the governance of their public institution is under the watchful eyes of the public and the media, and because of legal requirements to file annual conflict-of-interest disclosure statements. Furthermore, many public boards fall under the vigilance of an ethics commission, or its equivalent, with substantial power to impose penalties for violation of the rules.

As for other differences, there are several. Public boards are more visible, and therefore much more accountable, to the general public. In most states their meetings are open to the public, except for narrowly proscribed topics such as litigation or collective bargaining. Depending on the public agency, meetings of the board may receive extensive media coverage, even live TV broadcast. Small towns too may cover various town board meetings by way of a local cable TV company. Private boards tend to operate in splendid isolation, unless a crisis erupts and forces public attention upon them. As a result, the private board has greater control over information about its deliberations and much more choice about what it disseminates to others. Even private boards, however, are beginning to broaden and diversify their membership and open up their proceedings in response to shareholder or constituent concerns.

There is often better balance in terms of gender or diversity on a public board because its constituency is broader—the public—and also because public scrutiny makes obvious and unacceptable any overly homogeneous composition. Private organizations are usually formed to promote a narrowly defined private purpose; partly as a result, they tend to appoint as board members people who are quite similar and share an affinity for this purpose. Public boards, by contrast, generally serve a purpose as broad as the public itself. Even where the public purpose is narrowly defined and the board's members have expertise in this area, some of the members of a public agency board may be citizens representing "the general public."

The governing bodies of public organizations also tend to be political in the sense that members appear to be influenced by the presence of the media or the public. Imagine, for example, how different the House of Representatives' debate on impeaching President Clinton might have been without live TV coverage or with no reporters present. Participation in a board meeting of a public agency may resemble subtle or not-so-subtle campaigning, and as a result the meetings of public agency boards generally last longer and accomplish less than those of private organizations. As a chief executive, I chafe at the long-winded posturing that often occurs in a board meeting as the evening hours lengthen. Private boards, by contrast, may (but not always) accomplish a tremendous amount of work in a short period of time. The level of trust appears higher; deals may be struck before the meeting; and there is no camera or reporter to play to, no audience to convince or to enjoin in the discussion. At the same time, however, the private board deprives itself of the benefit of other points of view that would be expressed by members of the audience, and this can be a loss (except after 10:00 P.M.).

What Really Matters

In my experience, the difference between how private and public boards conduct their business is not the critical issue. What is most important is who serves on the board—and especially who serves as chair.

There are seasoned and able men and women on the boards of both public and private agencies, committed to the organizational mission and experienced in working effectively as a board. Although they are often selected because they are leaders, these people have learned how to work effectively as equals and colleagues on a board. Indeed, being a good follower may be the greatest skill of all. They come to meetings prepared, share the work to be done, and (ideally) limit their participation to moments when they can add real value to the issue under consideration. Such board members recognize that compromise is a necessity, and they also understand clearly the difference between the role of a member of the board and that of the chief executive officer.

The presence of such people is the determining factor in the organization's ability to govern itself wisely and accomplish its purposes. The board meetings of the directors of a private organization can be highly political and contentious; board meetings of a public agency can be focused and efficient. What matters most is the people, and their expertise and ability to function effectively in the task at hand.

Particularly important is the role of the chair. In more than a quarter century of work as the chief executive officer of two public school systems, two private colleges, and a private business corporation, as well as a past or present trustee of twenty-seven public or private organizations, I have worked with many board chairs. The success of each board—be it of a public or a private organization— depended far more on the leadership of the chair than on whether the organization was public or private. A good chair is absolutely critical to effective board governance of any organization or association, public or private.

Working closely with the chief executive, a strong board chair shapes an agenda and guides the board members toward decisions. He or she designs processes for examining an issue that are inclusive, yet focused and timely. Usually the chair tries to forge consensus among differing points of view; most often this is in reaction to recommendations prepared by the chief executive officer and staff. Strong board chairs can control public participation and guide it to effective means of expression (and do likewise with renegade board members as well). Strong chairs also recognize that consensus is not synonymous with unanimity; they know when to take a vote and move on.

From Aristotle to de Tocqueville

Boards are here to stay. Although Aristotle argued the benefits of a philosopher king as governor of the state (or, by implication, the head of any complex enterprise), the propensity to form a group, as discerned by de Tocqueville, has become a permanent part of American life. Our culture relies heavily on both public and private associations of all types to accomplish every imaginable civic purpose. Indeed, the huge number of such organizations, as well as the balance between them and the opportunity they offer for service on governing boards, is essential to the strength of American democracy.

I suspect that most board members do not understand fully the civic importance of their role. In participating as a trustee, director, commissioner, or other type of governing board member, a citizen is both advancing the specific purpose of the association and making democracy work by participating in self-governance (or conducting the public's business). As de Tocqueville recognized a century and a half ago, it is important work, worth recognizing and commending for its civic virtue.

Note

1. Tocqueville, A. de. *Democracy in America.* (H. Reeve, trans.). New York: Oxford University Press, 1947, p. 319.

DANIEL S. CHEEVER JR. *is president of Simmons College, Boston. He is a former superintendent of schools and has been a trustee of many public and private organizations.*

The author describes lessons he has learned as a superintendent of schools and concludes that educational leadership requires far more than applying textbook definitions of policy.

3

Lessons in leadership

Irwin Blumer

WHAT MAKES A LEADER? What makes a superintendent of schools a leader?

My children thought they had the job all figured out. The superintendent cancels school when there is a foot of snow, signs memos and diplomas, and attends some night meetings.

When I became a superintendent, I knew my responsibilities were more complex, but I struggled to define the essence of the role until I thought about the critical building blocks in the educational lives of children. The true role of a superintendent is to create values for the school system.

Clear Values and Leadership Traits

What do I mean by values? Values are beliefs and attitudes that shape and sustain the work of all the members of the school community. The superintendent identifies the three or four core values that are so strong—in both intellectual and emotional content—that they have the power to drive the people, the culture, and the

NEW DIRECTIONS FOR SCHOOL LEADERSHIP, NO. 12, SUMMER 1999 © JOSSEY-BASS PUBLISHERS

decisions that touch everyone in the school community. The superintendent cannot define these values by sitting at a desk. Establishing values is an active process, one that blends several important leadership traits:

1. Knowing yourself
2. Listening to and respecting others
3. Motivating others to work together with you for the common good
4. Accepting responsibility
5. Thinking long-term
6. Communicating often
7. Being persistent

Knowing Yourself

You cannot become an effective leader unless you know what you believe. Who are you? What do you care about with passion? What do you believe is important? What do you stand for? What do you want your school system to stand for? As an educational leader, how do you incorporate these principles into the beliefs of your school system? How should you work with your school board and others to develop a set of shared values for your schools? How do you motivate others to join that effort and to accept ownership of these principles?

These are key elements. Working with others, you can create a vibrant community upon beliefs that are strong enough to withstand inevitable pressures. You can establish and retain a sense of integrity. You do not need a cult or charismatic leader. You do need commitment to the idea that all children can learn and that all children are entitled to safe, effective, challenging, nonracist, and nurturing schools and communities.

It is ironic that we seldom raise questions of who we are and what we value with current or future school leaders. When such questions do arise, we rarely afford the time or settings to explore the ideals that drive our own best behavior. We should not, there-fore, be surprised to encounter superintendents who appear to be indecisive or arbitrary.

A clear set of beliefs and values does not make life easy for a superintendent, but life does become clearer for everyone else. People begin to sense the logical consistency of the values under-lying specific decisions. People learn that decisions do not change as a result of personality or political climate. Instead, actions are true to the superintendent's and the school community's values. Establishing this kind of integrity does take persistence, and at times a little courage.

If I were your mentor, I would advise you to have strong faith in yourself and stand up for what you value. Consider an example. In my first superintendency, the chairperson of the school board enjoyed a reputation for driving everything and everybody—her way or no way. My predecessor had acquiesced to her frequent directives and bombastic behavior. Shortly after I became superin-tendent, she asked to meet with me to discuss issues at the high school. Teachers and administrators were planning to revamp the course weighting system to encourage students to enroll in advanced, rigorous courses. Too many students were electing easier courses to ensure a high grade point average. Rather than explain her concerns or seek my assessment, she simply told me what she expected should happen. I explained that the staff had volunteered to design a plan and I would not superimpose her plan. I respected both their expertise and their commitment. Obviously angered, she stormed out of our meeting.

In the past, whenever similar incidents occurred the former super-intendent would later agree, reluctantly, to do substantively what she wanted. I chose to ignore her behavior and simply continued with my normal work. This choice was risky for me as a first-year super-intendent. I did not have long-term allies to balance against her posi-tion on the school board and within the broader community. In one sense, this was a classic power struggle. But the struggle was not about my ego versus hers—and that is an important distinction. The conflict was based on values. Respect for educators was a basic value that I held, and I expected school board members to honor and share it. Once she recognized the depth of my commitment, she backed away from confrontation.

Listening to and Respecting Others

Having faith in yourself does not mean that you can ignore the advice of others. If you want other people to own goals and values, the best way to motivate them is through a sense of shared responsibility. As a leader, you must listen carefully to ideas and criticisms from others.

Our school district embarked on a multiyear review of student performance on various national standardized tests, curriculum content, and course enrollments. The effort involved staff at all levels: teachers, curriculum specialists, building principals, and parents. Preliminary findings suggested that course content and expectations for students were not sufficiently high. Students were capable of better performance, as well as broader and deeper learning. Even though the dictionary definition of *rigor* carried a negative connotation, I pushed the idea with the school board, faculty, and parents that learning should challenge both students and teachers.

In response, a group of parents proposed programs for "gifted" students. In many school systems, similar proposals were easily accepted and implemented. Essentially, such pull-out programs served selected students, but there was little or no impact on the larger student population or on the content of their courses. I met with parents and staff members and explained that if we were seriously committed to the belief that all children can learn, we had to address the issue of the integrity of the academic program in a way that would benefit a larger number of students. Rather than channel a few students into rich and demanding education, we worked to gain the full support of parents to reconstruct a curriculum with higher content levels and higher expectations. Staff members also worked together to examine how they might enrich and strengthen expectations of themselves and their students. One significant change was the determination that all students should enroll in first-year algebra by grade eight. This led to restructuring the math curriculum throughout the school system, as well as retraining teachers in content and methods.

The point of this example is that given some basic values shared across the school community, people were willing to move away from positions that simply advanced their own interests. They began to assume responsibility for advancing the interests of others. In this case, the value of all students having a right to a rigorous academic program, the value of the centrality of the classroom, and the value of shared decision making and ownership all interacted to change the direction of education.

Motivating Others to Work with You for the Common Good

Our staff was concerned that African American students were not enrolling in the more challenging courses and were not achieving at a high enough level. Staff members presented a report to the school board that was published in the local media. The first steps called for the adult community to define the problem and accept responsibility. Rather than excusing this as a student, parental, or societal problem, staff members began to address what they as individuals and what we as a school system could do to change the patterns. We made a serious commitment to keep our goal of improvement for these students visible to the entire school community, and on everyone's agenda every day.

"Respect for human differences" was one of the core values adopted by the school board for the system. As was the case with other core values, each school annually defined an action plan to respond to this value. These school-based plans were submitted to the school board and were the basis for evaluating the performance of individual building leaders. As superintendent, I met weekly with the administrative council (all principals and central office administrators). Each month we devoted a full meeting to discussing our

progress to breathe life into our core values, with particular emphasis on our work to improve education for students of color. The lesson here is that serious commitment to a goal requires the leader
to develop structures that make a goal visible and keep it active.
Persistence is essential.

We also funded staff members' enrollment in semester-long programs developed by Jeff Howard and the Efficacy Institute. Efficacy education is founded on the principle that all children can
learn and that effort—not intelligence—is the key to success.
Teachers and other staff must develop high expectations for all children and help them achieve. Rather than a one-shot, one-year
effort, the system expected participation from key members of the
teaching staff in all schools, building administrators, and central
office personnel. In addition, we supported "training of trainers,"
so that teachers would offer courses to others and serve as role
models and mentors in their own schools. Staff members began to
evaluate their own methods of teaching, materials, and expectations
for themselves and their students. Over time, these efforts did
attain some improved achievement for African American students.

As part of our progress evaluation, several staff members of color
suggested that we should address the issue of racism. We might
have remained comfortable cloaking the problem in euphemisms.
However, from our concern for the students, staff discussions,
review of research, and the commitment of staff members to move
forward, we opened the door to confront the most difficult problem our country faces. With the help of Beverly Daniel-Tatum,
who has researched and written several articles and books on
approaches to active antiracist environments, our staff members
began to dig deeply into ways to change the climate for our students and staff.

The lesson here is that the superintendent as a leader has to listen to the voices of teachers and other staff members. As the leader
of my school community, I have an ethical and moral obligation to
act on those values I hold passionately, and to help others do so as
well. I could have simply said that the community, the school
board, the parents, or the other staff members were not ready to

talk about racism and its impact on students' lives and achievements. One teacher remarked that he understood that he had really adopted the principles of active antiracism when he found himself waking up in the morning thinking about what he could do that day. Having adopted respect for human differences as a core value, the school board endorsed this phase of our work, engaged in a miniworkshop, monitored action plans, and made a point of commending staff members for their contributions.

Accepting Responsibility and Promoting Mutual Trust

Superintendents gain credibility for their beliefs by accepting responsibility. Our community faced a complicated redistricting problem because we were opening another middle school. Sixth-graders would move from fifteen elementary schools to three middle schools. Those of you involved in redistricting understand the dynamics (people who have complained about a particular school for years cannot imagine their children elsewhere). After months of data gathering, analyses, defining options, discussion, and open meetings, I was prepared to offer the final staff recommendation, which I submitted to the school board in writing in advance of the public meeting. We expected a large turnout that night to hear final pleas from the community and to witness the school board discussion and vote.

On the afternoon before the meeting, the assistant superintendent of schools came to see me, visibly upset, after discovering an error in the data that invalidated the recommendation I was about to present to the public. I notified the school board chair before the meeting and informed her of the data error and its impact. I then accepted complete responsibility for the problem and offered to submit my resignation. When the public meeting began, I announced that there was an error in the numbers upon which we had based our recommendations, and that this would prevent the committee from acting on my recommendation that night. Accepting full responsibility for the error, I requested the community to direct all questions or comments about the matter to me—and not to any member of my staff.

We ultimately resolved the redistricting problem. But there was another lesson. I assumed public responsibility for the error and held myself accountable. That action amounted to a tangible definition of accountability for administrators, teachers, students, parents, and community members. I would not put somebody else at risk in public. I was not speaking about the responsibility for a command structure in the usual sense. I was speaking to the value of respect for one's colleagues and mutual trust. No organization is healthy where there is even a hint that members might be used as scapegoats to protect leaders. Although the school board was concerned about the error and possible repercussions, it refused to consider my resignation or any other negative action.

Thinking Long-Term

One community I served frequently invoked work-to-rule conduct if negotiations with teachers did not yield an agreement prior to the expiration of an existing contract. As a means of putting pressure on the school board and mayor to resolve open issues, union leaders advised the board and the public that teachers would perform only required duties. School boards and unions often disagreed about which responsibilities were a regular part of a teacher's job. In the public sector, teachers did not have a legal right to strike. As the end date of an existing contract passed, both sides became more frustrated. On one occasion, "back-to-school nights" became the battleground. The union held that these were voluntary meetings and that the teachers would not attend. Some school board members were adamant that back-to-school nights be held and that some punitive action be taken against absent teachers. The board planned to meet in closed session to make its final decision, and it was clear that a majority of its members wanted to force the issue.

When I entered the meeting, I faced a choice. One option was simply to keep quiet, let the board vote its wishes, and then try to carry out their directives. The school board conducted negotiations and, in this district, the superintendent was not an active driver of the process. However, I could not adopt a passive, accepting role because I envisioned the destruction of trust between parents and teachers if parents arrived for evening meetings that teachers refused to attend. Dividing teachers from parents would have both immediate and long-term negative consequences. So at the beginning of the school board session, I asked for one more opportunity to express my views and recommendations. I literally pleaded with the board to back away from this confrontation and allow us to postpone back-to-school nights until the contract could be settled. My argument was persuasive enough to change some votes, and we narrowly avoided a public battle between the teachers and the school board in which parents would have been caught in the crossfire.

Thinking and acting with a long-term, larger perspective can come with a price, though. Some animosity toward me lingered among members who were outvoted because I had intervened and affected the vote on the back-to-school-night question. Some relatively routine matters became more contentious. Yet once again, the value of centrality of the classroom was strong enough, even in a stressful situation, to drive the school board's ultimate decision to back away from confrontation.

Communicating Often

I also learned that even though a superintendent can have a clear, strong vision of content and climate for each and every student, until others share that vision there is no progress. One cannot influence or lead by memo. As superintendent, you need to work with others to develop joint ownership for the core values of the system. I identified several groups of others for this ongoing effort: the school board at bimonthly meetings, the communitywide parent-teacher organization council at monthly sessions, and the school administrative council (especially principals) at weekly meetings. You must never forget the fact that children attend individual schools. For tangible change and effective results, you must start at the school level, rely on the principal, and promote his or her skills and commitment.

In addition to scheduling regular visits to individual schools and classrooms, I moved quickly to strengthen the administrative councils. The council members included all the principals as well as key central office staff members. I made sure that managers of major initiatives such as METCO (Metropolitan Council for Educational Opportunity, a voluntary, state funded, interdistrict busing program) were council members to demonstrate my commitment to the success of such efforts. This was important evidence that they were all an integral part of the system because they had a seat at the table where decisions were made.

Administrative council meetings were held each week early in the morning, and every matter of importance to the school system was brought there for debate and discussion. At those meetings we defined common beliefs and expectations for common behavior. Our rules were quite simple. Though I chaired the meetings and was clear about which decisions or recommendations I would ultimately define by myself—as opposed to those subject to group debate and consensus—my role was primarily to listen and let others speak. Staff members did not feel compelled to speak at any meeting or on any topic. On the other hand, we all interpreted silence to mean agreement. Once everybody had an opportunity to speak, the group expected each member to honor the decisions. The feedback from these regular meetings was invaluable to my effective leadership because the administrative team—functioning as a team—informed my decision making. Despite all the conflicting demands on team members' time, their participation in these meetings helped to improve the entire school system far more effectively than would have been the case with less consistent or fewer face-to-face opportunities to communicate.

The council used these meetings to flesh out the four core values of the school district that drove every decision the system made about budget, annual superintendent–school board goals, and annual school improvement plans for each building: (1) centrality of the classroom, (2) respect for human differences, (3) collegial behavior, and (4) communication. There was never any question that individual schools would address all four core values, but they had total discretion about how to advance a particular core value. The people closest to the children—their principal, teachers, and parents—were best able to generate effective ideas for those youngsters. The core values served as a covenant, binding each school community together within itself and as an integral part of the community at large. Systemwide commitments, combined with the supporting plans from individual schools, constituted a cohesive set of priorities and direction for the school system. We could all speak a common language based on a common set of values.

Roles and Responsibilities: Policy Versus Implementation

Textbooks on superintendent–school board relationships advise an aspiring superintendent and his or her school board to define roles and responsibilities by separating "policy" from "implementation." In this neat world, policy rests with the school board, and the superintendent manages implementation.

Throughout my career in education, as an experienced superintendent and as an elected school board member I have not been able to function according to these rules. Rather than seeing clear distinctions, I always saw blurry lines. What might be policy in one setting is administrative responsibility in another. Consider these situations:

- Is development of a K–12 curriculum review process a policy matter warranting detailed consideration by the school board, an administrative responsibility of the superintendent of schools, or a combination of both?
- If a school district wants to implement block scheduling at the high school, is this a policy decision for the school board? Is it an administrative responsibility to be carried out under the direction of the superintendent of schools, in concert with the high school

principal, staff, and student and parent communities? Is it a responsibility delegated to the high school principal, staff, students, and parents, involving the school board or superintendent?

- Redistricting is generally regarded as the responsibility of the school board. In towns and cities with student assignment plans, school committees ultimately vote to establish new school boundary lines. Is this a pure policy decision of the school board? Does the committee simply choose to implement specific plans that were researched and proposed by the superintendent and staff?

My point is that trying to box school board–superintendent relationships into a policy-versus-implementation grid is simpleminded. Instead, we need to evaluate the nature of a particular problem in context and then, if necessary, separate the responsibilities of the committee as a whole from those of the superintendent. On the surface, such a process may appear messy, yet it is actually less legalistic and more realistic, and it should lead to mutual respect and cooperation between the school board and the superintendent.

Most important, once the school board members and the superintendent reach agreement on the larger questions of values, there are a set of three or four guiding principles. As a result, the amount of time and energy that a superintendent spends in educating and persuading the board on specific problems should decrease significantly. Each member is able to view questions in the context of shared goals and priorities.

Lessons Learned

Many of the skills that aspiring superintendents think they need to develop are somewhat mechanical. You can learn to communicate. You can learn to work with governmental bodies and with the school community. You can learn to devise an effective budget and to develop a clear policy manual. These are necessary tools. But just as skill in the laboratory does not make a great scientist, acquiring skills by itself does not make a great superintendent and educational leader. You need to learn some lessons:

1. Examine who you are and what you value.
2. Integrate your responsibilities as an instructional, administrative, and values leader.
3. Educational excellence, academic rigor, and student achievement are your responsibilities, whatever else you do.
4. Act on the principle that learning should present challenges to all children and that all children can and will learn. It is the responsibility of the adults of the school system to ensure that this happens.
5. Lead the way as a champion for the value of diversity and antiracism to ensure a healthy environment and high achievement for each and every student.
6. Work with others to develop mutually defined and shared core values.
7. Share decision making with others, particularly school principals and other members of your leadership team.
8. Transfer ownership and responsibility for advancing values and goals to staff, the school board, and other influential people in your community.
9. Develop a process for two-way communication, particularly with your leadership team, to ensure effective input from staff and parents and solid review of every important issue facing you and your school board.
10. Promote sharing, mutual respect, and collegial actions among staff members to improve curriculum and instruction—time, money, and continuous attention to content and methods.
11. Champion classroom teachers and their students as the primary beneficiaries of the resources available to the school district.
12. Be persistent.

The examples I have shared in this chapter illustrate my conviction that if you do not know who you are and what you believe, you cannot be an effective leader. People look to their leader for consistent beliefs and behavior. If you, the leader, are uncertain or unclear, there is no reason for people to trust you, and without trust there is no mutual vision. There can be no progress toward achieving common goals because there is no agreement on common goals. There may be some honeymoon periods, when a superintendent might assume that there are common values and goals, but through experience and observation I have learned that these periods do not last. A true leader takes the time to explore his or her own values and works to develop and articulate shared goals across schools and school groups.

References

Blumer, I. "The Principal as Instructional Leader." In M. F. Hayes and I. K. Zimmerman (eds.), *Teaching: A Career, a Profession.* Wellesley: Massachusetts Association for Supervision and Curriculum Development, 1999.

Blumer, I. and Tatum, B. D. "Creating a Community of Allies: How One School System Attempted to Create an Anti-Racist Environment." *International Journal of Leadership in Education,* 1999, 2 (3), 255–267.

Sergiovanni, T. J. *Moral Leadership.* San Francisco: Jossey-Bass, 1992.

Tatum, B. D. "Talking About Race, Learning About Racism: An Application of Racial Identity Development Theory in the Classroom." *Harvard Educational Review,* 1992, 62 (1), 1–24.

Tatum, B. D. *"Why Are All the Black Kids Sitting Together in the Cafeteria?" and Other Conversations About Race.* New York: Basic Books, 1997.

IRWIN BLUMER *is research professor at Boston College Graduate School of Education. He was formerly superintendent of schools in the Newton and Concord/Concord-Carlisle Regional School Districts, Massachusetts.*

The free flow of information between superintendents and boards needs to be woven into the fabric of the school year.

4

Communicating with the school board: Some practical observations

Mark C. Smith

YOGI BERRA IS SAID to have observed that one ingredient for a successful baseball manager is the ability to keep the players who don't like him away from the players who haven't made up their minds. In times of frequent turnover among chief school administrators, it is not difficult to translate this aphorism into a comment about the relationship between superintendents and school boards.

The issues that challenge superintendents and school boards probably have more potential for discord than those affecting baseball managers and players. Unlike a baseball team, members of a board of education may differ on what constitutes winning. The test of an effective superintendent is often the ability to bring five, seven, or nine board members together rather than keeping them apart. A critical ingredient in achieving consensus is effective communication with the whole board.

Shortly after my first appointment as a superintendent, but before assuming my duties, I sought advice from several experienced superintendents about working with the school board.

NEW DIRECTIONS FOR SCHOOL LEADERSHIP, NO. 12, SUMMER 1999 © JOSSEY-BASS PUBLISHERS

From two successful superintendents, I received diametrically opposed advice on one aspect of communication. One urged regular individual contact with each board member. The other advised that individual contact be minimized and that whenever possible I should communicate with the board as a whole. After twenty years as a superintendent, I have found that the latter is the wiser course of action. When superintendents share information in writing or in person with the whole board, they reinforce the fact that its deliberations and decisions are a group activity and that all members receive the same information. Importantly, they also reduce the potential for members to perceive favoritism in dispersion of information or attention from the superintendent.

There are many components to effective and meaningful communication, including concepts that are philosophical or value-laden such as honesty, openness, respect, trust, and integrity. There are also components involving more esoteric goals. Contrary to Berra, I spend a considerable amount of time wrestling with ways to use communication so I can bring together board members who have divergent views. In this task of drawing in those with opposing convictions and strong opinions, I am often reminded of Edwin Markham's wonderful poem, "Outwitted":

> He drew a circle that shut me out
> Heretic, rebel, a thing to flout.
> But love and I had the wit to win:
> We drew a circle that took him in![1]

This chapter, however, is neither philosophical nor esoteric. It focuses on four practical vehicles with which a superintendent can build and maintain effective communications with a school board. One vehicle is a well-thought-out and designed weekly communication to the whole board. The other three involve private, in-person communication with the full board. The in-person communication, of course, has the added dimension of being two-way.

Weekly Communications

In my experience as superintendent, a well-organized, thoughtfully written weekly publication, *Communication*, has been one of the most important vehicles of good communication to the whole school board.

Several factors are critical to ensuring that it has a positive impact on the board in terms of process and content. First, it is published regularly in a consistent, well-organized format. Each issue is dated and numbered. I reserve the use of salmon-colored paper exclusively for the weekly newsletter. This distinguishes it from other material that may be included in the packet. The board also understands that information on the salmon notes is privileged.

Second, it imparts timely information. *Communication* has a calendar of meeting dates and times for the coming weeks and information about the schools. Before public or executive sessions, it includes background information and discussion of items on the meeting agenda, and I also enclose copies of letters received or sent, pertinent memos, and articles of interest from newspapers or journals. My salmon notes regularly offer comments on the attachments, and sometimes I insert my own opinion piece on national, state, or local issues to stimulate board members' thinking about issues.

Third, it offers insight into the superintendent's role. Members of a school board often do not have in-depth knowledge or understanding of a superintendent's job beyond our role in public meetings and other visible decision-making arenas. *Communication* is a good vehicle for sharing information about the superintendent's routine weekly activities. Brief notes about meetings, school visits, and professional activities can, over time, give board members a realistic understanding of the nature and demands of the superintendent's position.

Fourth, it highlights accomplishments and maintains good morale. An important purpose of *Communication* is to give the board a weekly dose of good news about students, school activities, and staff members. By including information on high test scores, impressive learning activities, outstanding individual accomplishments, and awards or recognition, the weekly publication helps board members feel good about the schools and gives them positive ammunition for informal discussions they may have with members of the community. Of course, it is also a place to report accurately on less-positive incidents and to address rumors that may be circulating in the community.

In his classic book about D-Day, historian Stephen Ambrose compares General Rommel's pessimism to General Eisenhower's efforts to convey enthusiasm and optimism. Eisenhower believed that optimism is a key factor in leadership. Ambrose quotes from a letter the allied commander wrote to his wife: "optimism and pessimism are infectious and they spread most rapidly from the head downward. . . ."[2] Although between a superintendent and school board the communication is upward rather than downward, Eisenhower's observation is equally true and worth remembering. The tone of your own publication should be upbeat, positive, and optimistic. I make it a point never to end *Communication* with something negative, and whenever possible I end with a positive note about students or staff, or at the least a light observation.

A hidden value in the weekly bulletin is the help it extends in orienting new members of the school board. My administrative assistant maintains three extra sets of *Communication*. When new members are elected to the board, their orientation materials include all the back issues of the current year's salmon notes. Since the notes offer concise reports, discussion, and comments on every recent event or issue of significance in the district, they give an excellent overview and background.

Preparing weekly salmon notes takes time. I prepare mine on Thursday night and Friday morning for delivery to the board on Friday. I have heard many superintendents say they do not have time to put out a weekly communique of five to eight pages. I say there is time for any activity that is a high priority, and good communication with the governing board is invaluable. It is worth the time. When done well and regularly, it quickly becomes an important vehicle for communication between the superintendent and the full school board. Feedback suggests to me that board members rely on and look forward to the salmon notes.

In-Person Communication

In addition to weekly issues of *Communication* for the full school board, regular in-person communication is critical to a good working relationship and sound decision making. Unlike the written communications, the two-way process of in-person communication has the advantage of direct feedback.

Along with regular public meetings, three more private forums offer superintendents important opportunities to speak with the entire board. The first is in executive or private sessions; the second is at planning retreats; and the third is during the annual sessions devoted to evaluating the superintendent's performance. All three are opportunities for communication in both directions. Done well, the annual planning retreat and the superintendent's evaluation are often linked.

Regular executive (closed) sessions offer important opportunities for communication among board members and between the board and superintendent, although open-meeting laws often restrict the content of discussions out of public view. The comparatively informal contact that such sessions afford fosters effective dialogue. To maintain cohesiveness, it is critical to prevent lengthy lapses between executive sessions, even if it takes some creative thinking to develop an agenda. Not to be overlooked also is the value of brief periods of informality and interaction while members are gathering and departing.

The benefit of bringing the school board together for regular private meetings with the superintendent became apparent to me when I moved from New Jersey to Massachusetts. In New Jersey, the board of education must act on each and every personnel item. Since we reviewed all personnel matters routinely with the board in executive session before listing them on a public agenda, there were always good reasons to schedule an executive session after every public meeting.

In Massachusetts, the Education Reform Act of 1993 awarded authority for virtually all personnel discussions (and many other responsibilities) to building principals and superintendents. Therefore, because these regulations limit decision-making responsibilities for school committees (and the open-meeting law is tough), weeks could pass with no reason for scheduling an executive session. Delighted with the opportunity to get home earlier than normal, I often did not schedule one. It soon became apparent, though, that committee members were distancing from each other and from the superintendent. No sooner did I recognize this than I began to "discover" reasons for private or executive sessions. Relationships and communication improved among committee members and between the committee and the superintendent.

However valuable the relaxed interactions of private or executive sessions can be for communication, they generally occur late in the evening and are often controlled by open-meeting laws. Offsite annual planning retreats offer a far better opportunity for good communication. With a well-constructed agenda, at a planning retreat committee members and the superintendent can engage in sustained discussion about concerns, objectives, and issues of interest to all. Even if such retreats are subject to open-meeting laws, rarely does the press or the public attend. In my twenty-year career in three districts, no reporter or interested citizen has appeared except in response to a specific invitation.

The ideal retreat is overnight and out of town, at a conference center or similar facility. Friday dinner through Saturday afternoon is a good time frame, allowing three lengthy work sessions (Friday evening, Saturday morning, and Saturday afternoon), three opportunities for a shared meal, and an informal social period (after the Friday night session).

If economics, public meeting laws, or the views of committee members preclude leaving town, try to identify a local site other than the committee's regular meeting room. Sometimes local businesses or churches are willing to contribute a conference room. If circumstances limit the choice to school property, then a library or faculty room can be a good change of scenery from the usual meeting room. A single all-day retreat on a Saturday is a reasonable alternative to the two-day plan. If the retreat is a single day, it is valuable to include a group breakfast and lunch in the planning.

The content of a planning retreat can and should run the gamut from brainstorming activities to guest speakers on key issues facing the district, and team-building exercises designed to help the committee understand group process and group decision making. It is not unusual on planning retreats for communication to be one of the topics on the agenda. Outside facilitators are often helpful for one or more sessions. A key to making the retreat as effective as possible is focusing on objectives for the coming year as well as group process, since both activities are difficult to accomplish in regular meetings. Furthermore, discussing these issues in a different, less-formal setting encourages greater satisfaction and resolution without the pressure of public presence or the need to take action.

Discussing objectives for the coming year (hopefully in the context of long-range planning) is a particularly worthwhile topic for the annual retreat. The identified objectives become one lens through which to shape the superintendent's annual year-end evaluation.

School boards must understand the complexities of education and the challenges of both short-term objectives and long-range planning. On more than one occasion, I have introduced a theory of MIT economist Lester Thurow, that one of the problems of American business has been our emphasis on short-term achievements at the expense of long-term gains. This is a good message for school board members when discussing objectives, and for politicians who seek to exploit the public's desire for a short-term fix rather than sound long-term plans.

One year, a colleague and I scheduled our planning retreats for the same weekend at the same conference center. We interspersed our board members at assigned tables at dinner and scheduled a speaker and follow-up discussion for one joint session. It was successful. One benefit was the insight gained through informal talk at dinner (where we purposely placed specific people together). Board members from both districts found that they faced similar problems. It is always helpful for boards in like communities to realize that their issues and frustrations are not unique.

The annual evaluation of the superintendent offers another opportunity for open, two-way discussion and communication about the district. However, in Massachusetts the opportunity is greatly hindered by the requirement to conduct the superintendent's annual evaluation in public session. Although it is possible to improve the process through a subcommittee format, doing so still limits the number of people who can participate in this important opportunity for two-way communication. In New Jersey, the law is exactly the reverse. The evaluation must be in private session unless the superintendent requests that it be public.

When I worked in New Jersey, I developed with my board a four-part evaluation process, including two private sessions devoted exclusively to the evaluation. These sessions, although sometimes painful, can be a unique opportunity for in-person communication with the full school board and offer the only time during the year that is purposely designed to give feedback to the superintendent. This feedback should include discussion of communication and its effectiveness.

If the superintendent's evaluation process is scheduled for the end of the school year and a planning retreat is scheduled around the start of the school year, both events—as opportunities for personal communication and discussion between school board and superintendent—can book-end the school year. In their own way, each can also lay the groundwork for effective communication throughout the year.

If the annual planning retreat includes development of district objectives for the coming year, the bookend schedule of these two activities also ties them together in content. The superintendent and school board communicate at the end of the year about the specific objectives that were developed in the planning retreat at the start of the year.

Concluding Comment

Communication is an interesting facet of the superintendent's job. Its treatment in this chapter is limited to four practical vehicles by which the superintendent can and should communicate with the school board. Practical processes for communication are mundane, not esoteric. They are, however, critical to the superintendent's success. Our task is not to keep committee members who are unhappy with us away from members who are undecided. Our task, rather, is to bring our five, seven, or nine committee members together within the circle. Communication is a means to that end. The very practical aspects of a well-organized and purposeful weekly publication and intelligent use of executive session, annual offsite retreats, and evaluation sessions can improve and support superintendent–school board communication.

Notes

1. Markham (1936), p. 67. Used with permission.
2. Ambrose (1994), p. 61.

References

Ambrose, S. E. *D-Day June 6, 1944: The Climactic Battle of World War II.* New York: Simon & Schuster, 1994, p. 61.

Markham, E. "Outwitted." *The Best Loved Poems of the American People.* (Selected by H. Felleman.) New York: Doubleday, 1936.

MARK C. SMITH *is superintendent of schools in Framingham, Massachusetts. Previously he was superintendent of schools in Chatham and Westfield, New Jersey.*

Despite the frustrations, the role of superintendent provides an unequaled opportunity to serve as a community's chief advocate for children. We need boards that recognize that a team relationship with the superintendent, based upon collaboration, is central to improving student achievement.

5

A view from both sides of the table

Harry A. Galinsky

THE RELATIONSHIP BETWEEN superintendents and their boards of education is frequently identified as an important measure of their career success. This issue, coupled with the increasing turnover rate among superintendents, has created major concern for the leadership of our public schools. Search consultants regularly report that the pool of highly qualified candidates for the position of superintendent of schools is very shallow. As a result, boards of education often make the difficult choice to restart superintendent searches because they cannot reach consensus on the finalists. Currently, in nearly forty districts in New Jersey retired superintendents are acting as interim superintendents. This situation, which exists in all types of districts—including some of the best in the state—presents a major challenge for public education. Without stable and successful leadership in the school districts across our nation, it is difficult to manage significant school change and reform. There are, however, some possible answers to the questions that are raised as this issue is discussed across the country.

NEW DIRECTIONS FOR SCHOOL LEADERSHIP, NO. 12, SUMMER 1999 © JOSSEY-BASS PUBLISHERS

As a former superintendent, I bring to this forum the insights gained from experience in two school districts over twenty years. I also have been active for twenty years as a consultant for many superintendent searches. In addition, I speak from my experience as a board of education member and president for the past five years. Superintendents must offer leadership and promote effective school reform, while also forging a positive and trusting relationship with school boards, many of which micromanage.

Ten Commandments for Superintendents

Though school boards bear a significant responsibility for the success or failure of their chief administrator, my suggestions here apply to superintendents because I believe professionally trained school administrators can face difficult situations and still create a climate of trust and community support in which they are then able to devote their energies to advocacy for children.

My version of the Ten Commandments for superintendents paves the way for building successful relationships with boards of education. In my role as school board president, I have seen how critical these suggestions are for the success of the superintendent, and so I offer them as a coherent approach to support superintendents who seek success.

Commandment One: treat each board member equally. This is often the most difficult commandment to keep. When one or more board members attempt to undermine the authority and success of the superintendent, the natural reaction is to seek the counsel and support of other board members who are publicly and privately supportive. However, not treating all board members equally is often used as a rationale by boards for seeking to oust the superintendent. Time devoted to the care and feeding of some board members must be shared equitably with all board members.

The *Second Commandment* to superintendents is that they give all board members enough timely information, and in a format that is easily understood and free of jargon, so they can act on proposals or recommendations.

Commandment Three calls upon superintendents to carry out with enthusiasm any action or policy of the board, even if it conflicts with their own recommendations. After an unsuccessful effort to influence the board about a given issue, any additional attempt to obstruct the impending decision is self-defeating. Superintendents expect their staffs to carry out their directives effectively, and boards expect similar follow-through. The superintendent who cannot do so should consider moving on to another district or career.

The *Fourth Commandment:* do not expect the board to support all your recommendations. The worst possible public perception of a board of education is that it is a rubber stamp. Full discussion and debate is healthy and necessary and allows careful review and analysis of important decisions. This is often time consuming but well worth the effort. Modified proposals often result, with improved likelihood of success. Discussion also serves as an important political opportunity for board members to demonstrate their independence legitimately. They want their constituencies to perceive them as informed and major contributors to the success of the district. Superintendents need to foster public opportunities for board members to help shape the debate on important issues.

Commandment Five deals with the issue of communication, a requisite skill for a successful and effective superintendent. Board members should be regularly informed of all highlights, both good and bad, especially between meetings. The community needs to view the members of its board of education as informed representatives who know enough to deal effectively with questions from the media, staff, parents, and the local citizenry. Nothing troubles board members more than being the last to know, which often leads to erosion of trust between them and the superintendent.

Making a recommendation, even one that may be unpopular, is the *Sixth Commandment.* If there is a controversial issue, the board looks to the superintendent for guidance and a possible solution. When the superintendent suggests options, the board members and also the public can see which alternatives were considered as a recommendation was developed. Lack of action by the superintendent in the face of contentious issues is sometimes seen as lack of strong leadership. Boards want to be shielded from the flack that frequently accompanies difficult issues, and they want the superintendent to deflect or neutralize the anger and emotions usually present in these situations.

The *Seventh Commandment* deals with developing a leadership style that evinces a sense of humor and calm despite the stress of events. The superintendent's personality or style sets the tone for decision making. A thoughtful, calm approach to controversy, coupled with judicious use of humor, often tempers major conflicts or battles. If the board president demonstrates similar virtues, the district has a formidable team in a crisis situation.

The ability of the superintendent to survive difficult conflicts with the board is the focus of the *Eighth Commandment*, to base all recommendations and decisions upon the answer to the question, "What is in the best interest of the children?" Following this advice may strain—or even terminate—the relationship between superintendent and board. It is critical, however, that school leaders observe this commandment faithfully if children in our public schools are to receive the educational opportunities they need and deserve. Leaving one district because of personal commitment to this commandment is often seen as strength by a board seeking a courageous leader and can lead to an opportunity in another district. It is a fact of life for superintendents currently, and in the foreseeable future, that doing what is right may mean moving on to other leadership positions a number of times in a career.

During a presentation at Teachers College, Columbia University, Carol Johnson warned, "If you are doing what you are supposed to do as a superintendent of schools, you will be alienating at least 10 percent of your constituency each year. After five years, you will have at least 50 percent of the community unhappy with you, and it may be time to move on." Obviously, frequent turnover of superintendents dramatizes the need for stability in leadership for a district with a long-term plan for growth and improvement. Isn't it possible to have educational leaders who make difficult and controversial recommendations in the best interests of children and who then survive? Fortunately, there are numerous examples of very successful superintendents who have made a difference in the lives of children and stayed the course over many years in the same school district. Those who continue to lead a school district successfully over a significant time span have learned the lessons of dealing effectively with their boards and the community. They regularly do things that create support and understanding of their vital role as chief school administrator.

The *Ninth Commandment* illustrates a leadership style that receives board, staff, and community respect and support. It says, "Be visible in your schools and classrooms and at major school and community functions." People need to know the leader of their schools. Keeping this commandment is time consuming and often intrudes on precious personal time for family and self. However, making this commitment often broadens the basis of support for the superintendent and overall public support for the schools.

Finally, the *Tenth Commandment* states, "Continue to grow professionally by reading and attending conferences and seminars, to be aware of current research and successful practice." Modeling this behavior is a major effort in support of the ongoing staff development activities in the district. We often talk about how important it is for all of us to be lifelong learners. The superintendent's own personal efforts in this area are critical in creating a climate for growth and change in our schools.

As the Board Sees It

The view from the board's side of the table focuses on the process that leads to positive superintendent-board relations. School board behaviors that create a climate of trust, respect, and support are essential to the success of the superintendent. To make the relationship work, boards can establish firm expectations for interaction and communication with the superintendent. They can demonstrate trust by not making assumptions; they can be prepared to compromise, clarify the meaning of *emergency*, and evaluate the relationship at fixed intervals. The superintendent's evaluation is the most under-used or misused opportunity for enabling continued success in the relationship. The board must clearly outline what it takes to get an A and should agree on the evidence that is the basis for its judgment. There must also be frequent opportunities for the superintendent to do what former Mayor Ed Koch of New York City did regularly: ask, "How am I doing?" When this happens with school administration, an overwhelming number of superintendents can and will meet a board's expectations.

Lack of clarity or changes in board priorities often lead to super-intendent-board conflicts, frequently dramatized by turnover among board members and resulting in a situation in which the majority of sitting board members did not participate in selecting the superintendent. Despite turnover, boards can maintain the orig-inal relationship by demonstrating an understanding that the super-intendent is the professional leader in the district. If the board respects the superintendent's right to be the educational leader and, at the same time, reinforces its policy prerogatives, the relationship works. Both parties should understand and assume that they will not always be friends, but the relationship must be based on mutual respect and understanding.

Board members need to know and understand what the super-intendent does. A process that orients them to the superintendent's daily activities and responsibilities is, therefore, important to the relationship. This should not lead to an urge to check up on the superintendent's daily activities; in fact, it should lead to under-standing that the day-to-day operation of the district is the respon-sibility of the superintendent.

The lines of communication must be open. It is the board's responsibility, usually through the president, to make certain the superintendent is informed of issues of concern to the board itself as well as the public. A no-surprises policy is as vital for the super-intendent as for the board. The established communications pat-tern should include regular opportunities for board participation in the planning process for the agenda and to discuss other ideas and priorities. These sessions often extend formal and informal feedback on goals. They also can answer Mayor Koch's question for the superintendent.

Building and sustaining a positive superintendent-board relationship is enhanced if both entities share the spotlight. Joint appearances to acknowledge accomplishment help to build the trust essential to the relationship. It is the board's responsibility to heed the credo to do nothing that makes the chief school administrator look bad. The board should be prepared to run interference, support the superintendent, and refrain from making remarks that reflect badly upon the person or position. Finally, when making difficult decisions, board members should not keep score or press the superintendent against his or her professional judgment. Good boards do not hide behind "The administration made us do it."

A board that operates according to the suggestions I have outlined in this chapter has every right to expect outstanding success from its superintendent, because it has eliminated the most frequently identified causes of poor job performance. Such supportive efforts give credence to the lyrics of an old song that says, "If you can't make it here, then you can't make it anywhere."

Although these suggestions can foster a long-term positive relationship between a board of education and its superintendent, this very complex relationship resists simple admonitions of what to do or not to do. Since I have been on both sides of the relationship, I can easily identify with the analogy of the relationship to a marriage. The problem with this analogy, however, is that even though both parties took vows to respect, honor, and even obey, the parties to the ceremony are changeable.

What does a superintendent do when the values and beliefs of the majority of the board no longer match his or her philosophy of education? This situation presents a challenge for a superintendent who has not been prepared to address conflict within the governance structure. Those who meet this challenge successfully understand that being in charge does not necessarily mean being in control, and they understand that their responsibility includes constant and systematic education of board members. They must engage board members individually and collectively to fully understand what motivates them to serve. More important, they need to determine their vision for educating children. Gaps in understanding one another can be bridged if people take the time to truly listen to each other and resolve differing points of view.

As a superintendent, I quickly learned that individual board members' behaviors changed markedly when they were part of the group in public from when they were alone with the superintendent. I did what many superintendents now do regularly: meet individually with each board member, particularly those new to the board, and focus on learning about each one's priorities as a board member. I used to ask, "After your service to this board, what would you like to remember as your greatest accomplishment?" (Of course, the superintendent needs to be prepared for someone who answers, "Getting a new superintendent.")

As president of a board, I often seek opportunities for members to meet with me and the superintendent informally. This helps the superintendent learn about our concerns and issues in a nonadversarial setting. Both the leadership of the board and the superintendent must encourage this relationship so that any communication gap can be closed, not necessarily to achieve agreement but at least to produce fuller understanding of issues. Public meetings do not lend themselves to accomplishing this goal, because for elected boards the politics of the election process itself often condone behavior that is not conducive to a basis of trust and cooperation with the superintendent.

Boards must understand that the departure of a superintendent—whether by choice or not—can be counterproductive. Changing the leadership in a school district may be seen by some as a solution to problems, but it may very well impede accomplishing system goals and increasing student achievement, both of which serve as the report card for the board and the superintendent. In the interest of stability and long-term school improvement, to reduce the turnover rate of superintendents a mechanism for conflict resolution must be in place, tailored for the relationship. No one specific process is successful everywhere, but agreement to have a process is critical, even when the relationship is excellent. It makes good sense to develop a plan while both parties are calm and objective. I believe that the mere presence of an agreed-upon process facilitates a positive relationship. Though other opportunities exist for conflict resolution, through state organization boards or superintendents, I do not believe that such external resources can be as effective as an internal process mutually agreed to by both parties before a problem emerges.

The analogy of marriage and prenuptial agreements seems to have a comfortable place in this discussion. It is more desirable to seek a strategy that promotes a positive relationship between a board of education and a superintendent than to prepare for conflict. I have identified school board–superintendent relationships as critical to improved public schools in the United States. A recent study published by the Educational Research Service, *Getting There from Here. School Board–Superintendent Collaboration: Creating a School Governance Team Capable of Raising Student Achievement* (Goodman, Fulbright, and Zimmerman, 1997), points out that true reform and increased student achievement are not possible until the quest for school improvement focuses on school governance. This study resulted in forty-one recommendations to improve school governance, which I have condensed into these six major strategies:

1. Build a foundation for teamwork. Establish a sound structure of governance with goal setting, planning, and high instructional standards. Involve the community in creating a vision for schools that allows students to develop to their maximum potential.
2. Get the best and most capable players. Recruit citizens for board service who put children first, and who are not immediately related to employees of the district. Elect board members to serve at large, and do not pay them a salary. Offer superintendents long-term contracts that provide competitive compensation and benefits.
3. Ensure that the team players know their roles and responsibilities. Boards should make policy and adopt budgets that sup-

port district goals. They should delegate administration of schools to the superintendent, including all such personnel matters as recruitment, development, evaluation, promotion, and dismissal.

4. Use team training. Offer orientation workshops for new board members. Ensure that boards and superintendents pursue continuous learning, with a special focus on collaboration for higher student achievement.

5. Adopt good team strategies. Conduct board business only as a committee of the whole, with no standing committees. Hold only one business meeting a month. Do not approve contracts for goods or services that might result in personal or financial gain.

6. Convince others to support the team. Form a blue-ribbon task force in each state to recommend improvements in superintendent certification, open-meeting laws, and legislation to support collaborative governance.

The vision of a collaborative relationship between the board and the superintendent needs to drive the efforts of state and national associations. We already know what it takes to forge an appropriate relationship. The question remains, "Who will take the responsibility to make it happen?" Superintendents are often given power, but they are rarely given the control they should have. Although the responsibility is shared, the ability and commitment to develop this vision rests with the board, and it entails willingness to give up control.

As I reflect upon my experiences both as a superintendent and as a board president, it strikes me that there is no other role in public education comparable to that of the superintendent of schools. Despite the mantle of leadership and all its trappings, it is a very lonely job. No matter how close one's associates, how supportive one's board, how understanding one's public and one's family, no one else can fully feel the weight of conflicting expectations, of demands that exceed resources, of the necessity to compromise between ideals and realities. One superintendent once said to me, "Some days I feel like the only adult in town." Yet the role provides an unequaled opportunity to be the chief advocate for children in the community. It is a bully pulpit to lobby for their needs and to speak out as a voice of reason on behalf of children.

The fate and success of public schools rest heavily on the ability of superintendents to exert leadership to make a positive difference in the lives of children. We need to develop awareness among boards that fostering a team relationship with the superintendent, with a basis in collaboration, is the most effective way to accomplish the goal of improved student achievement. This is the challenge that faces public education. Our ability to meet that challenge successfully may very well determine the future of public education in this country.

Reference

Goodman, R. H., Fulbright, L., and Zimmerman, W. G. Jr. *Getting There from Here. School Board–Superintendent Collaboration: Creating a School Governance Team Capable of Raising Student Achievement.* Arlington, Va.: Educational Research Service, 1997.

HARRY A. GALINSKY *is senior fellow at the New Jersey Institute for School Innovation and president of the Bergen County Board of Special Services. He has served two New Jersey school districts as superintendent and more than twenty-five school districts as a superintendent search consultant.*

*New Hampshire's commissioner reflects on the con-
flicts and cultural shifts that have characterized
development of educational policy in the state.*

6

Cultural change at the state level

Elizabeth M. Twomey

WHEN I MET THE STAFF of the New Hampshire Department of
Education, but prior to my appointment as deputy commissioner
by the State Board of Education, the first question asked of me was,
"Do you think that citizen boards of education have any place in
the life of a department of education or of a local school board?"
The questioner was clearly asking on behalf of the other staff members. It was equally clear that, given the state of the relationship
then existing between the "education community" and the state
board, the hoped-for answer was a definite no.

This—and subsequent encounters with department staff, with
the education organizations outside the department, and ultimately
with the board of education itself—served to confirm my view that
a condition existed that could only be described as a breakdown due
to irreconcilable differences. Each side did not listen to the other,
was not civil to the other, had no respect for the other, and had a
totally opposing belief system as to how and under what conditions
children should be educated. At the time of my entry into the
department, it was difficult to determine which was the chicken and
which was the egg.

NEW DIRECTIONS FOR SCHOOL LEADERSHIP, NO. 12, SUMMER 1999 © JOSSEY-BASS PUBLISHERS

Over time, I came to believe that there was enough responsibility to go around for the breakdown in the various relationships. In my view, no one group was exempt from that responsibility. I do not believe that a fundamental joining of the minds could have occurred, given the political climate and the professed ideology of the state board at the time, but a different method of communicating on the part of the principals from all sectors might have helped to assuage the vitriol that accompanied every board meeting and public discussion for the next eighteen months.

The composition of that particular state board of education in its belief and action, and in manifesting members' personalities, was considered to be extreme by most observers (with the exception of a small but highly vocal group of citizens, including, not insignificantly, the state's largest newspaper). The board's discussions and subsequent policy positions and votes did not appear to demonstrate commitment to public education. Its public treatment of the then-commissioner of education, along with members' rudeness and obvious disdain for those from the educational ranks who had preceded them, served to reinforce the view of the majority of people that this was a board committed to serving a narrow agenda. At the least, this approach trivialized and polarized the serious issues confronting the state; at worst, the method blocked true advancement.

The New Hampshire State Board of Education numbers seven members, appointed by the governor, but the terms, which span five years, do not run concurrently with the appointing governor. Selection of five members is from five designated regions of the state. Two other members are appointed at-large.

When I became deputy commissioner, four members of the board appeared to be more amenable to dialogue than the remaining three. The commissioner asked that I be the interface among himself, the department, and the board. I was new, I had no "baggage," and I had had previous experience with some challenging boards. He believed his own relationship with the board members to be past saving; yet there was another year or so to pass before he would complete his term of office.

Upon observation, and as a result of a number of conversations, I noted that there had been little planning for or structure in presenting topics at a board meeting. There was a cyclical process of program presentations with no context for presenting them, and little understanding of the implications of these presentations to the process of education or the goals of the board and the education department. Although this was in part deliberately determined by the staff—an attempt to obfuscate what they knew to be controversial in an effort to continue the work—one result of this approach was that the board members had the impression they were not being given all the facts or an understanding of the implications of their taking action on any given topic. These board members were bright people, experienced in their own professions, and they knew that there was a disconnect between what they were hearing in the presentations and what their experience and instinct told them was true.

After a series of lengthy (and usually turbulent) discussions with the staff, we set out to prepare for board meetings by thorough dialogue and by revising the packet sent to the board prior to each meeting. We painstakingly talked through the issues in a series of board briefings, to crystallize the issues and help diminish fear among staff of the actual board discussion. To win staff cooperation, they had to believe that the work on which they expended their passion and effort would not be subject to harm through exposure to the board. The commissioner stood apart from this process. He offered no objection to it, however.

The consistency of this approach, over time, resulted in lifting the oppressive atmosphere at board meetings. It did not, of course, change the fundamental beliefs of the presenters or the board members. But it did result in the type of dialogue that expanded communication between the two, and it did enhance the credibility of the staff with the board, which came to believe it was receiving all necessary information on a given topic before a vote was required.

It is important to note that the board did not vote as one mind. On numerous topics three or four members would attempt to moderate both the discussions and the votes. They did not in any circumstance prevail.

Context

Many states hold strongly the belief that their form of governance is local control. In New Hampshire the belief in, and adherence to, local control goes deep into the soil and soul of the state. One native of New Hampshire, a fine man and someone who has had a significant investment in and concern for the state all his life, told me that "to a citizen in this state, 'the state' is as far as he can see from his back porch." To have the state capital, Concord, attempt to dictate to the "village citizen" is as onerous to him as the dictates of Washington, D.C. The culture of the state is laced with this libertarian view of life: "I got mine; you get yours; leave me alone." The Common Good view of life is not part of the landscape. As a way to preserve this view, the legislature consists of 424 members in the House and 22 members in the Senate. The office of the governor is distinctive in what it can prevent, not in what it can initiate. This governance approach was deliberately designed to keep control in the hands of the individual towns and cities, particularly as represented by the House membership, the third largest governing body in the free world.

To buttress this view, education funding in New Hampshire has been almost solely the responsibility of the local town. Until 1998, 97 percent of the financial support for education came from local property taxes.

When one combines the state culture with the method for funding education, it is not difficult to understand why the citizenry resists any kind of commitment to "dictates" from Concord. Additionally, the people believe they know best concerning the education of their children. "What was good enough for me, is good enough for them" is the comment that superintendents and principals of schools most frequently hear from parents.

Change

A number of factors came together to begin what is proving to be a sea change in the culture of the state.

Demographics. While recovering from the depression of the 1980s, the state experienced an influx of population into its southern tier. This geographic area is below Concord and abuts Massachusetts. More than seventy thousand people travel south from New Hampshire to Massachusetts to work each day, but they are attracted to live in New Hampshire because it is less populated, it is free of income tax, and the purchase price of a home is more affordable. (In one such community alone, two hundred children have moved into the town every year for six years.)

Over time, the new population began to seek the same services available to residents of Massachusetts. The new residents also discovered that their property taxes far exceeded their previous property taxes, though their houses were not worth as much on the real estate market.

Although there are only one million people in the state of New Hampshire, well over half of the total population lives in the southern tier.

Lawsuit. In 1992, five school districts sued the state in what would come to be known as the Claremont lawsuit. The plaintiffs charged that the right to a free, public education is a fundamental right of the children of New Hampshire, and, further, that it was the duty of the state to provide that education as defined in the state constitution.

The State Supreme Court remanded the case to the Superior Court. There were two lengthy trials (Claremont I and II). In both trials, the Superior Court found in favor of the state. The plaintiffs appealed to the State Supreme Court.

On December 17, 1997, the State Supreme Court found in favor of the plaintiffs. Further, it directed the governor and the legislature to find a solution to the inadequate funding problem that was "proportional and fair across the state." The court further said that the definition of adequacy of education had to include those components that would prepare a child for the next century and the global economy.

Political Factors. In the early history of the Claremont lawsuit, the state had a conservative Republican governor and legislature who chose to address the lawsuit by ignoring it—except by excoriating the Supreme Court and its decision. The only statewide newspaper, widely perceived as ultraconservative, continued the drumbeat against the court and for the right of local governance and decision making. Much was made of the need to preserve "the New Hampshire advantage." In 1994, the State Board of Education elected me as commissioner upon the retirement of the previous commissioner. (In New Hampshire, the commissioner of education is the only officer not appointed directly by the governor.)

In 1996, a Democrat was elected governor. She had campaigned on the issue of education (installation of kindergarten, in particular) and lower electric rates. She was previously a state senator and had a reputation for being honest, fair, and a problem solver. Her election changed the tone of the public debate on education. In the course of her first two years in office, she had the opportunity to replace almost every member of the State Board of Education, either on expiration of term or their choice to resign. Those who resigned were influenced by the fact that the previous chairman of the board had been the new governor's opponent in the race for the governor's office.

In 1998, for the first time in eighty-two years, the election produced a Democratic senate. The changes in the office of governor, senate, and state board of education not only altered the way in which the Claremont lawsuit was addressed by the state but also dramatically changed the relationship between the State Board of Education and all its constituencies, not the least being the Department of Education and my office as commissioner of education. The new members of the board were open supporters of public education. As such, they were highly regarded by various public constituencies. The concerns they expressed at public meetings addressed such matters as whether or not there was a high enough standard, sufficient resources to reach a quality standard, and enough emphasis on the "professionalism" of the teaching profession. The Department of Education staff began to alter its view of the role of a public board of education.

The Role of the State Board: 1996

As with most sea changes, total and substantive change takes time. The entire composition of the state has not changed. There is no sense of total agreement and singleness of purpose on the issues of education (or anything else for that matter!). But the stake has been put in the ground.

The legislature has passed a bill authorizing a new way to fund education in the state. The state contribution is now nearly 60 percent of the total cost—not 3 percent. There is dawning recognition that if the state wishes to remain competitive, it needs an educated workforce, and we cannot afford to leave any child behind.

One of the first questions the new chairman of the state board asked me was, "How can this board be of help to the department?" He wanted to know how we could enhance each other's roles while respecting our differences. We expanded this discussion to include other board members and senior staff at the department. The conversations set the course and direction, the goals and objectives for both entities over the next few years.

Perceived as supportive of public schools, this state board has gone far in restoring the faith of the public in this governmental body. As such, it has also changed the perspective of department staff as to the value and support of such a lay board in advancing mutually held goals.

Reflections

A lay citizen board formed to assist policy setting for the public schools is not a new concept. Well over 150 years ago, de Tocqueville called attention to the fact that when Americans proposed to advance some truth, or to advance a civic purpose, they formed a group of like-minded citizens.

My experience in Concord, New Hampshire, requires me to emphasize the notion that the group must be of like mind to be accepted by those who look to it for direction. Certainly, a citizen board appointed to advance the cause of an institution must believe in that institution if it is to be viewed as a leader by the constituencies it is supposed to be serving.

In the case of the state board of 1992, although its values and beliefs coincided with those of the governor at the time and a small minority of the population of the state, its lack of faith in and support of the very public schools over which it had regulation-making authority caused the board to be largely ignored by local districts. When it was not ignored, it was publicly repudiated. Because the board did not support the public schools, the staff of the department of education felt justified in "building the catacombs" through which they funneled their programs. This was necessary for their own survival and to ensure that federal dollars and assistance would get to the schools. The mentality was that of an army of resistance in a cause believed to be just. It was a classic them-against-us approach to life.

Because of their experience, the members of the 1992 board could not see the benefit of a lay board committed to public education. The former chairman of the board was dedicated to advancing her views, without regard to the needs or thoughts of the local school districts.

When the new board developed in 1996, department staff began to see potential in a collaborative relationship with a board whose goals (if not individual objectives) paralleled their own. They watched cautiously while a new board chairman consistently and coherently expressed support for public education and consensus building. They grew in confidence as they witnessed the new board members expressing their own support and their desire to work collaboratively with the variety of associations and citizen groups who supported public schools. They have become critical friends and thoughtful, trustworthy participants in the myriad issues with which a board deals in these times.

As commissioner, I have been given a level playing field and a sounding board of substance. We do not always agree. But we always respect one another's views. We are all headed toward the same destination, although our routes may vary. They do not require me to be a savior, and for me that is very fortunate. They understand the political, public process, and they have knowledge and even savvy about the workings of organizations.

As well, they and their predecessors have confirmed in my mind a number of things:

- One cannot work long in a place where the prevailing values totally differ from one's own.
- Change can happen quickly; but sustained growth takes time and the commitment of like-minded people.
- Mature, competent people who are committed to the mission of the organization they serve can make a significant difference in the lives of the people they serve.

Without this focus on the mission, the organization finds its ability to govern wisely and achieve its goals severely compromised.

Life in Concord is still in tumult. Among other things, change is hard. It does not immediately lead to the promised land—nor does it vanquish all adversaries. But in Concord, the change has been supported by a board whose eyes are focused on their vision—and whose commitment is evident to all. And that has made all the difference.

Reference

Tocqueville, A. de. *Democracy in America.* (H. Reeve, trans.). New York: Oxford University Press, 1947, p. 110.

ELIZABETH M. TWOMEY *is commissioner of education in New Hampshire. She was previously associate commissioner of education in Massachusetts and superintendent of schools in Lincoln, Massachusetts.*

A large and diverse regional high school tackles disparities in academic achievement between white students and students of color. Greater candor in public discourse offers a glimmer of hope.

7

Minority student achievement and public discourse

Allan Alson

THE STORIES ARE INDELIBLY imprinted in the hearts and minds of the African American community. Mere mention of their details stirs the anger and disbelief that accompanied the original insult. Explicit messages, plainly spoken, told African American children that they could neither achieve nor aspire to the same goals as white children. Painful episodes repeated over time with but slight variation afforded the black community little trust or confidence that their schools would be fair to their children.

Our community, once a stop on the Underground Railroad, has long had an historical black community. Like the community, Evanston Township High School (a single-school district with a contiguous elementary feeder system) takes pride in the diversity that defines our population. In the nine years that I have been here, the racial demography has changed little. In 1998–99, for example, 46 percent of the students were white and 42 percent African American. The rest of the students were 7 percent Latino, 3 percent Asian, and 2 percent multiracial. Of the 30 percent of students

NEW DIRECTIONS FOR SCHOOL LEADERSHIP, NO. 12, SUMMER 1999   © JOSSEY-BASS PUBLISHERS

on the free and reduced lunch, nearly 90 percent of those were African American and Latino.

I vividly remember recounting to an audience stories I had heard of our teachers and counselors telling black children they were not college material. At the end of the talk, an elderly black man approached me and said with tears in his eyes that in the 1930s that had indeed been his experience. Though he had gone on to college and had a successful career, this practice and its insidious variations persisted at least through the mid-1960s. Lower expectations for black students are now communicated in much more subtle forms . . . usually.

In late January 1992, three students in the hallway disrupted a teacher's class. When the teacher opened his door, he discovered that three African American boys were the cause of the noise. Frustrated by the interruption, he returned to his class and made a strikingly outrageous racist remark in front of his students. One student, a multiracial boy who had been very fond of this teacher, bolted from the class and reported the remark to an administrator.

From this single remark, a journey fraught with danger was begun. Not surprisingly, word about the classroom incident began to spread throughout the school and community. Students, staff, parents, and community members spoke among themselves, hoping to learn the particulars of the event. Unfortunately, no official word of factual circumstance and response was provided. Though the teacher did receive a brief two-day suspension without pay, there was no statement from the administration decrying the utterance, and certainly no strong declaration against the evils of racism.*

The first general public awareness was generated by a flyer placed in staff mailboxes by the Students Against Racism club. Within days there were student protests, including a brief but remarkably peaceful walkout. African American community lead-

---

*Author's note: At the time of the incident, I was the assistant superintendent for curriculum and instruction. Our superintendent denied my urgings and those of fellow administrators to inform staff and community. This unexplainable lack of action by this otherwise very good man remains baffling today.

ers came to school to lodge their vehement response and to speak with students and staff. Of course, the media descended upon the school.

One week after the flyer appeared, the school board met. This was the first meeting since the teacher had made his comments. Forty-six speakers addressed the audience with great emotion. Public sentiment seemed to fall into three general categories. One theme was utter outrage and a strong demand for the teacher to be fired, along with an equally strong demand that the school finally rid itself of all vestiges of racism. Another more moderate stance was the call to learn from this incident and seek greater understanding through workshops and town meetings. Not lost on the crowd was the third sentiment, shared by a few students, teachers, and parents, who stuck by the teacher for the respect and admiration he had previously earned for his instruction.

Within days, the superintendent announced a plan to hold a series of town meetings to address racism and its effect on learning and the general school operation. Three raucous meetings took place, each attended by about three hundred people. There was tremendous anger, some of it dramatically displayed, which in turn provoked the deeply held resentments of the African American community. Many whites were alarmed by the disruptive nature of the meetings and worried about the implications for the future of this school, which held a strong reputation as a top-notch academic institution. Eventually, the negative energy displayed at the town meetings was channeled into a set of committees.

The policy committee produced an excellent set of nondiscrimination policies that were adopted by the board and remain the framework and criteria by which we judge behaviors. They extended beyond race to include all aspects of discrimination. A committee on school climate inspected school policies and practices and determined there was no evidence of unfair application of the school's discipline code.

Another committee, which addressed academic issues, found a number of problem areas. Concerns about counseling, postsecondary preparation, and ability grouping yielded the dramatic (though not surprising) extent to which African American students were performing very poorly compared to their white counterparts. The committee acknowledged that although the reasons for poor achievement varied, the consequences were quite evident.*

I led this last committee, called Ability Grouping and Tracking. The tension in these meetings was palpable. Equal numbers of whites and blacks were in attendance. It is important to note that neither whites nor blacks spoke with one voice. Many whites felt that any threat to tracking was in fact an attack on high standards and the school's commitment to strong academic achievement. A large number of blacks heard this fear as support for the status quo. Actually, as it turned out, very few blacks advocated an end to tracking. Instead, they called for greater access to honors and AP levels, and academic support for their children. However, the dialogue often obscured the common goal of academic success that parents held for their children.

The way I heard them, the exchanges went something like this:

AFRICAN AMERICANS: We've got to get rid of tracking—it's keeping our kids from achieving.

WHITES: If you get rid of tracking, standards will go down, and we won't send our children here anymore.

AFRICAN AMERICANS: This is just a cover for not wanting your children to be in class with our children. See, this is about race, not learning.

WHITES: This has nothing to do with racism and everything to do with achievement.

As Thomas Kochman wrote in *Black and White Styles in Conflict* (1981), differences allow for cultural experience and misunderstand-

---

*The school used (and still uses) three levels for academic grouping of students: honors, level two, and level one. Juniors and seniors may take advanced placement (AP) courses, seen as yet another academic level. The proportion of African American students in honors classes hovered at 20 percent and was only slightly more than half that number (12 percent) in AP courses. Courses at these higher levels were given "weighted grades," enhancing the opportunity for students to attain a higher class ranking—and further compounding the problem of racial disparity.

ing of intent. I concluded that I heard both sets of parents caring deeply about their children and arguing for the same goals. In truth, the strategies for achieving these goals were actually quite similar.

Both groups eventually acknowledged that honors and advanced placement courses offered the academic rigor and challenge they wanted for their children. Both agreed they were fearful that the other levels were not as demanding, therefore producing inferior education. Whites clearly stated their anxiety that "opening up" the honors classes might diminish standards and that resources allocated to boosting achievement of "others" would limit expenditures for the "high-end" academic programs. On the other hand, African Americans also explicitly felt that honors courses held the key to their children's success, but they believed the school needed to remove the artificial barriers that stood in their way.

When the recommendations from the Ability Grouping and Tracking Committee reached the board, two were notable for the responses they elicited. One proposal was to develop strategies to ensure full implementation of existing policy, allowing parents to have final say in placement of their children. The board was upset that more parents were not exercising this right and insisted that the administration find ways to inform and support parental choice.

The other recommendation proved more problematic. Originating from the history department, teachers proposed that all U.S. history courses (except AP) become mixed-ability-group classes. Initially, the board was quite skeptical, believing that standards would fall and these classes would not be sufficiently rigorous. What won the day for this proposal was teacher tenacity. They designed an intricate system of academic support, including new text materials, lunchtime tutoring by college students, and extensive opportunities for teacher planning. Despite the fact that this proposal was about racial equity for honors-level material, the discussion itself rarely touched upon race. Its politeness and focus on teaching and learning obscured the genesis of the issue. One is left to wonder whether framing the conversation outside of race enabled it to become acceptable even as race was on the minds of all involved.

A fascinating debate about race-based program initiatives was intertwined into the recommendations from the Ability Grouping and Tracking Committee. Six years prior to this racially charged situation, the school had created a program intended to boost "minority enrollment in honors classes." STAE (Steps Toward Academic Excellence), which continues to thrive, enables promising freshmen (based on test scores) to enroll in honors algebra or geometry and honors English. Students receive intensive summer work, special study-hall tutoring, and extensive weekly monitoring. Parental involvement is also an essential component of the program. Students remain in the program through their sophomore year.

To this day, there is debate among board members about the original intent of the program. Each year statistics presented to the board include a racial breakdown of the students. Black students have made up 45–55 percent of the STAE program over its twelve-year history. These numbers effectively increase the overall percentage of African American students in honors classes. However, the notion of a program devoted only to students of color is problematic in our diverse school and community. Most board members contend that any quality program should be open to all eligible students. Other board members contend that unless the school dramatically increases STAE's minority enrollment, there will not be a significant increase of students of color in honors classes. The discourse on this issue used to be quite heated, often getting stuck on divergent opinions about the program's original purpose. Now, with the same players making the same points each year, it is as if each person has already played out the dialogue before it begins. What feels frustrating, I think for everyone, is the unwillingness to broach the risky waters of whether there should be race-based programs and, if so, what they should look like.

The board and administration have significantly and very publicly stepped up the pressure to improve minority student achievement. Since 1992, numerous reports have been made to the board on various aspects of achievement of students of color. Each department is responsible for creating and evaluating initiatives annually. What is painfully evident is that our African American and Latino students significantly lag behind their white peers in all measures of achievement. Whether the analysis is grades and class rank, state assessments, or college acceptances, the results look the same. When reports or program proposals come before the board, the dance of language offers a valuable perspective on how very tough it is to talk about race. A few examples illustrate this difficulty.

Four years ago, the administration was approached by a group of black parents requesting that we consider raising the minimum grade-point average for participating in extracurricular activities and interscholastic athletics. As it turned out, this issue divided the black community in a way that caught white supporters of the idea off guard. The divide among African Americans, though not strident, certainly demonstrated contrasting points of view. Advocates for the increase in minimum GPA believed very strongly that students would live up to raised expectations. Opponents worried about increased numbers of ineligible students, who would lose activities of interest and become further disengaged from their schooling.

Both sides agreed this was about black kids, since they made up the greatest number of ineligible students. To me, it seemed that many whites who initially liked the idea of the grade-point increase wavered when some blacks cast their opposition. Did "liberal" feelings cause sympathies to transcend what at first seemed like a simple academic imperative? Board members explicitly stated they believed this was an initiative that would improve minority student achievement when they unanimously cast their votes in support. It is important to note the board voted to phase in the new standard and to add study tables and a part-time academic advisor for ineligible students. Obviously, they took their work seriously and have reaped the rewards of virtually no increase in ineligible students.

Another venture had a much-less-public beginning. The Boosters Club offered to fund an ACT prep class for athletes who needed support in their motivation and preparation for college. We proposed a variation: that the class be solely for African American and Latino students who scored in the low midrange on the PLAN (Pre-ACT tenth-grade test). The club's officers (one white and one black) raised their eyebrows and questioned our comfort level with this approach. Now, after two cycles of the course, the enrollment has more than doubled to forty-nine students. We have presented reports about the course to the board. Somewhat surprisingly, there have been no questions raised about this race-based approach by either the board or those reporters who regularly attend the board meetings. Given that there are other opportunities for students to take an ACT prep course in other after-school venues, does silence in this case connote approval, or does it simply mean no existing resources are threatened? I must admit I have not raised the question, perhaps fearing the answer would close down a promising program. This venture has not prompted public questions, but a summer school course proposal certainly did.

Sometimes the best-intended efforts have confusing results. To what extent can we design initiatives that serve predominantly minority populations? A new summer school course in precalculus was proposed in the fall of 1998. This course had been reviewed and approved by our Curriculum Council, comprising all department chairs and most administrators. The course proposal explicitly stated that its primary purpose was to build minority enrollment in calculus. At the board level, questions were raised about the availability of this course for all students. Although the answer was that all students could enroll, a special effort would be made to recruit students of color. The course was approved and offered for the first time during the summer of 1999, and teachers encouraged minority students to enroll. What puzzles me is not knowing what elements of this course raised concern. Is it possible that a high-level academic course feels like a scarce resource to be protected? In truth, we all danced around our inner thoughts to secure the desired political ends. Maybe this was a win-win result, but what price will be paid by avoiding the deeper issues?

Two recent endeavors have struck a favorable chord, perhaps by identifying an acceptable euphemism: initiatives designed for students who come from families with little or no college experience. In one case, we introduced a program that is being used across the country: AVID (Advancement Via Individual Determination), which serves middle-level students through a class structured to build motivation, organizational skills, and interest in college. More than 75 percent of the thirty-six freshmen who enrolled the first year (1998–99) were students of color.

In addition, we added a new staff position, college application specialist. In this case the same rubric as that used for the precalculus course carried the day. All students would be served, but strategies would be employed to reach students from families with little or no college experience. Both AVID and the college application specialist have gained support at all levels in the school. In the case of AVID, it may be easier to extend resources to midlevel students if high-achieving students necessarily seek the same support. As long as all students have access to the college application specialist, there is likely to be no controversy.

Finally, the board truly took the lead in pushing the administration to find a way to record and report student achievement over time. We all recognized that grades, stable assessments, and even ACT or SAT scores measured trends with different cohort groups. As is true for most schools, there was no system in place for reporting and analyzing how well the same students were doing over time. Adopting a longitudinal assessment system would be one way to take a careful look at the academic growth of all students, and in particular the achievement gains of students of color. Recently we adopted such a system, using a series of highly correlated ACT tests to be administered in the eighth, tenth, and eleventh grades. This new strategy may yield the data and subsequently the platform from which explicit conversations about race and achievement can be held.

To reach our current stage of dialogue and action, certain conditions had to be established. Clearly, the first was public pressure, which constituted the necessary precursor to mobilize a response from a large public institution. Over time, the school district has demonstrated its willingness and capacity to state equity goals clearly and articulate a credible set of steps designed to actualize these goals. The issue has remained front and center for the district's public agenda. If not, both public and staff might legitimately question the district's commitment.

The public exhortations and expectations from the school board have called for realistic plans with time lines for action and scheduled periodic progress reports. In our case, it has been incredibly helpful that the school board has had great stability. In addition to a low turnover rate, board members actively seek replacement candidates who share the same basic values and commitments. In this instance, the values include willingness to publicly discuss race, examine achievement from a variety of perspectives (not just test scores), listen carefully to staff initiatives, demonstrate respect for staff concerns, and persist in prodding for improvement.

Two points seem key. In public, the reliance for information is derived from staff, students, and the public, not just the superintendent. The board is genuinely interested in knowing what the various constituencies see as the conditions for success as well as the barriers that might preclude improvement. Second, the board makes clear its desire to see advancement through a wide variety of indicators. Although board members, of course, care deeply about bottom-line numbers, they let others know that they do not believe the numbers alone tell the whole story.

As superintendent, I have found that the board's trust in me depends on my full candor about problems as well as successes. It certainly has taken time to develop relationships where we each believe in the commonality of purpose and strategies. This comes from constant communication and a long-term focus on the same overall goals year in and year out.

The board wants to be convinced that its superintendent is serious about the issue of minority student achievement. It receives evidence through relentless public messages, program initiation and review, and ultimately public feedback that a real effort is being made and results are being felt.

I believe, in large part, that we have reached our current stage of openness about race and achievement through pressure, persistence, shared values, and continuity of leadership.

Certainly, the long-term deleterious effects of racism are never far from the surface. The goals of minority student achievement, and explicit and public recognition of the existing disparities between white students and students of color, now shape the discussions, planning, and program evaluation. Though progress is slow and steps forward are sometimes taken too gingerly, the course for public action has finally been established. Unfortunately, longstanding fears and mistrust continue to impede the discussions of minority student achievement. However, great candor in public discourse provides a glimmer of hope where before there was none.

Reference

Kochman, T. *Black and White Styles in Conflict.* Chicago: University of Chicago Press, 1981.

ALLAN ALSON *is superintendent of schools in the Evanston (Illinois) Township High School, District 202, where he was previously assistant superintendent for curriculum and instruction. He is a former high school principal in Reading and Scituate, Massachusetts.*

School leaders often have more freedom and leeway than they use because the very pressures that are driving people out of the field increase the leverage of those who remain.

8

The authentic leader: Surviving and thriving in difficult times

Robert Evans

AT A CONFERENCE not long ago, I came upon two superintendents sharing a moment of bemused pleasure. Each had been contending with a critical school board; one had recently been called—in public session—"barely average." But then each had been invited to apply for openings in nearby communities, with sharply increased salaries, whereupon each was offered a raise by his own board to keep him from applying elsewhere. "We may be 'barely average,'" said one, "but as long as we can stand the abuse we're in demand." Indeed. A search consultant recently told me that if he is seeking a high school principal or superintendent, he now feels lucky to attract thirty applicants for positions that previously drew seventy-five or eighty. And as I write this, the headline in *Education Week* is about the continuing sharp decline in the numbers of candidates for principalships nationwide.

The collapse in the number of educators interested in running schools and districts highlights an enormous irony about school leadership: we have never known more about it than we do today,

NEW DIRECTIONS FOR SCHOOL LEADERSHIP, NO. 12, SUMMER 1999 © JOSSEY-BASS PUBLISHERS

yet school leaders at all levels have never felt more stressed and vulnerable. In the scores of schools and districts I visit each year, most of the administrators I meet say they love education, like leading, and can't imagine doing anything else, but they add that the quality of their life is deteriorating. They find themselves working harder than ever, and longer than ever, and at a more sophisticated level, yet subject to more criticism and second-guessing, and they feel increasingly at risk in their jobs. When they gather at professional conferences, their conversation is increasingly marked by frustration, cynicism, and gallows humor. And they are voting with their feet, turning away from careers as school leaders.

The Context of Concern

At first, all this negativity might seem odd. After all, in the past few decades we have learned an enormous amount about leadership; several thousand books have been written about it, several hundred about educational leadership alone. Administrators are better trained than ever; more of them have doctorates then ever. And there is much that is encouraging in the ferment about school reform that we have come to call "restructuring," with exciting advances in our understanding of how children learn, ways to enrich instruction, and so on.

But we have only to look a little further to understand school leaders' rising distress. Many of the educational improvements envisioned are vast and complex. Schools are being pressed to make enormous leaps in curriculum and instruction, integrate technology into their operations and instruction, revamp their modes of assessment, decentralize their governance, fulfill ever-expanding special education mandates, and address accelerating social problems. Even if each of these changes is compelling on its own, an opportunity to do enormous good, collectively they are often far beyond a district's fiscal and human resources.

These rising expectations for schools also occur amid a climate of deep distrust: pronounced loss of institutional authority throughout America, suspicion of officials and organizations, and assertion of individual autonomy, rooted in the political turmoil of the 1960s and 1970s. This climate has helped to foster unprecedented criticism of schools. Most recently, this has been reflected in a national frenzy over accountability. States have rushed to impose high-stakes tests (the instruments themselves hastily and often badly designed) to prod and threaten schools to improve rapidly or risk serious consequences (loss of accreditation or funding, transfer of teachers and principals, state takeover, etc.).

All these changes have a negative impact on administrators directly, and on the teachers they lead and the board members to whom they answer. Across the country, principals report growing demoralization among faculty. Problems of communication and morale, and of resistance to change, particularly among veteran faculty, are widespread. Since school administrators lack the staffing clout that corporate leaders enjoy—they can't just replace low-performers—they must innovate with their existing staff, no matter what its level of energy, competence, and enthusiasm. This means that the complexity of leading change is not just technical but motivational, something altogether more difficult.

Staff distress and dysfunction are frequently mirrored at the board level. As districts have been buffeted, board membership has grown more draining and less rewarding, leading to frequent turnover. Where once a superintendent could expect to work for six or seven years with a majority of the board that hired him or her, today this interval may last only three years. Loss of continuity brings loss of perspective and means that decisions are often not so well informed. It can also mean that board members are less able to tolerate bad news or the time it takes to correct problems. Any report of staff inadequacy or programmatic weakness can loom large. A common response is to intensify monitoring and intervene directly—micromanaging, as we have come to call it. Boards exhaust their superintendents in frequent, lengthy meetings and with demands for endless amounts of information about daily details and management decisions.

Reviewing these and other leadership stresses, I have suggested elsewhere that a candid advertisement for a superintendency or principalship would not begin "We seek a dynamic leader with a world-class vision for the twenty-first century . . ." but as follows:

Wanted: a miracle worker who can do more with less, pacify rival groups, endure chronic second-guessing, tolerate low levels of support, process large volumes of paper, and work double shifts (seventy-five nights a year out). He or she will have carte blanche to innovate but cannot spend much money, replace any personnel, or upset any constituency.

The Technical Fallacy Versus Authentic Leadership

In the face of all this, the chief response has been to intensify training of administrators, hoping that greater management expertise will enable them to address the ever-growing range of tasks they are assigned and problems they encounter. States and professional associations now require lengthy lists of skills and competencies for administrative certification. Leadership training is a growth industry. In its most common forms, it aims to turn leaders into masters of both the big picture and the immediate situation. But even though it includes much talk about the "strategic" parts of leadership, it typically emphasizes the tactical ones. Most administrator training concentrates on a long list of techniques that are to be matched to each situation, individual or group, as needed. It focuses on leadership "styles," urging leaders to learn how to adapt their styles to those of others.

Clearly, a school leader needs technical expertise in a range of areas; he or she wouldn't survive a day without a repertoire of maneuvers. But trying to rely primarily on technique is enormously self-defeating. It gives the leader yet more to do—acquiring these techniques is itself an additional burden. It fosters the stress-inducing expectation that a good leader can—and should—be all things to all people. It ignores the reality that none of us can significantly change our style. Worst of all, it submerges the leader's most important assets—his or her core commitments and natural strengths—and reduces the leader to following everyone else.

This kind of leadership training omits a key point that management experts in the corporate world have recently been making: leaders of high-performing organizations are not "style masters"; they tend to be people of strong character with strong commitments who maximize their strengths. They are by no means all similar: some are intensely hands-on, others are great delegators; some don't hesitate to criticize poor performance, others accentuate the positive; some care mostly about basic skills, others about higher-order ones. What they share in common is self-knowledge and commitment. To study these leaders is to realize a truth with tremendous liberating potential: there are many ways to lead successfully. In fact, there is no approach to leadership that does not have both strengths and weaknesses, and the two are almost invariably linked; we can't have the strength without the weakness. Thus the key for a leader is not to chase some ideal—a composite list of virtues from the management bookshelf—but to be the best of what he or she is. This does not mean doing what one pleases and never learning or adapting. It means concentrating on one's strengths and, when necessary, compensating for one's weaknesses. It is what I think of as authentic leadership.

Purpose and Conduct, Clarity and Focus

What does authentic leadership look like in action? This is a much larger topic than I can cover here, in part because it varies depending on the commitments and personality of the leader. But whatever their differences in philosophy and approach, authentic school leaders almost always concentrate on two essential features of school life: purpose and conduct. They work to build and sustain consensus about what the school stands for and what it means to be a member of the school community.

Authentic leaders know that true community cannot exist without shared values and shared norms for behavior. At the school level, the key custodians of these values and norms are the faculty, led by the principal; at the district level, the board, led by superintendent. I think of these groups collectively as the school system's "providers." They need to clarify and then assert the school's basic purposes and core commitments—not just its program goals, but the principles that guide it. (What kind of school (or district) are we? What is distinctive about our approach to education? What are the conditions of membership in our community?)

Clarity of purpose means coalescing around a few truly central values, not a long list of virtues and wishes of the kind that fill the typical school mission statement. There is nothing wrong with listing all the qualities to which a school or district aspires, but doing so rarely motivates or sustains anyone's effort. What does motivate and sustain is clear affirmation of values that actually matter to the people who must implement them, that proclaim not just goals they should aim for but commitments and strengths they already share. These values may be clarified through a collective process, but they must be actively embodied by a leader in words and deeds. This does not require charisma and eloquence (though they surely help!), but it does require commitment and consistency from a leader who proclaims, defends, and exemplifies the values.

Authentic leadership that builds outward from core commitments and personal strengths offers a useful model for creating shared understandings and mission among a school or district's providers: strengths first. Much of what is so draining and demoralizing in education today stems from a chronic focus on defects and shortcomings. But it is always easier to build on strength than to attack weakness. Providers can best create meaningful, motivating mission if they begin by cataloguing their strengths and skills (and those of their students and parents) and seeking ways to nurture, extend, and apply them to their challenges and weaknesses. This is an ideal way to sharpen a school's sense of purpose and its providers' morale.

The other essential feature of school life—conduct—refers to behavior and responsibilities. Authentic leaders insist that core values apply to everyone, not just students, that the values translate into norms for behavior and responsibility for all members of the school community. Although most schools have expectations for students, the best have expectations for all their participants, including faculty, staff, board, and parents. Thus, if respect for others is one of a school's core values, the school cannot simply preach and teach respect to students. It must expect all the adults in the school community—faculty and parents alike—to model respect and hold each other accountable for doing so. Similarly, from the very top of the district on down, the superintendent, board, and administrators must themselves exemplify the respect in how they treat one another and the other members of the school community.

Being clear about purpose and conduct has important implications for school improvement efforts. It calls for focusing priorities, not a smorgasbord of programs. Most districts' improvement agendas, as noted above, are overloaded and underfunded, lists of projects that may be compelling individually but are unrealistic in the aggregate and in their time frames. No organization, even a wealthy one, accomplishes five or six innovations simultaneously. One great source of cynicism about school reform is its long history of improvements that never reach completion.

Administrators and boards need to enable staff to concentrate their efforts by identifying a few clear priorities to receive adequate attention, support, and follow-through. This is essential, but hardly easy. Saying a clear yes to some priorities means saying a clear no, or not now, to others. Making the case for their priorities is a key challenge for all school leaders; fortunately, it comes naturally to the authentic leader.

All well and good, you may be thinking, *but how would I actually get away with some of this?* The answer, like the problem we began with, involves sharp irony: as the pressures on leaders grow, so do the opportunities to assert leadership. Of course, no leaders are free to do just as they wish, especially in a public school; all must bend and compromise and adapt. But none are rewarded for abandoning their key priorities, or for scurrying endlessly to be all things to all constituencies. Their opponents don't give in more easily the next time out of gratitude (on the contrary, they just push harder), while their supporters lose heart and find them more difficult to follow.

The truth is that most school leaders have more freedom and leeway than they use. In part this is because the very pressures that are driving people out of the field increase the leverage of those who remain. But it is also because asserting strength builds strength. People everywhere—all of us, teachers, board members, and parents—long to be well led. Not bossed, led. The current climate of school life makes the need for leadership greater than ever. Authentic leaders focused on purpose and conduct are uniquely ready to answer this need in a way that inspires confidence, builds common ground, and gives schools a fighting chance to master the challenges they face.[1]

Note

1. For more on authentic leadership, see Evans, R. *The Human Side of School Change* (1996); Kouzes, J., and Posner, B. *The Leadership Challenge: How to Keep Getting Extraordinary Things Done in Organizations* (1987); and Vaill, P. *Management as a Performing Art: New Ideas for a World of Chaotic Change* (1989), all published by Jossey-Bass.

ROBERT EVANS, *a clinical and organizational psychologist and consultant to schools, is director of the Human Relations Service, Inc., Wellesley, Massachusetts.*

Index

Back Issue/Subscription Order Form

Copy or detach and send to:
Jossey-Bass Inc., Publishers, 350 Sansome Street, San Francisco, CA 94104-1342
Call or fax toll free!
Phone 888-378-2537 6AM-5PM PST; Fax 800-605-2665

Back issues: Please send me the following issues at $25 each.
(Important: please include series initials and issue number, such as SL8.)

1. SL _____

_____

_____

$ _____ Total for single issues

$ _____ Shipping charges (for single issues **only;** subscriptions are exempt
from shipping charges): Up to $30, add $5^{50} • $30^{01}–$50, add $6^{50}
$50^{01}–$75, add $7^{50} • $75^{01}–$100, add $9 • $100^{01}–$150, add $10
Over $150, call for shipping charge.

Subscriptions   Please ❑ start   ❑ renew my subscription to *New Directions
for School Leadership* for the year 20___ at the following rate:

❑ Individual $52   ❑ Institutional $105
NOTE: Subscriptions are quarterly, and are for the calendar year only.
Subscriptions begin with the spring issue of the year indicated above.
For shipping outside the U.S., please add $25.

$ _____ Total single issues and subscriptions (CA, IN, NJ, NY and DC
residents, add sales tax for single issues. NY and DC residents must
include shipping charges when calculating sales tax. NY and Canadian
residents only, add sales tax for subscriptions.)

❑ Payment enclosed (U.S. check or money order only)
❑ VISA, MC, AmEx, Discover Card #_____ Exp. date_____

Signature _____ Day phone _____
❑ Bill me (U.S. institutional orders only. Purchase order required.)
Purchase order #_____

Name _____

Address _____

_____

_____

Phone_____ E-mail _____

For more information about Jossey-Bass Publishers, visit our Web site at:
www.josseybass.com   **PRIORITY CODE = ND1**

OTHER TITLES AVAILABLE IN THE
NEW DIRECTIONS FOR SCHOOL LEADERSHIP SERIES
Rebecca van der Bogert, Editor-in-Chief